STEAM ON THE ROAD

DAVID BURGESS WISE

HAMLYN

LONDON·NEW YORK·SYDNEY·TORONTO

CONTENTS

Published by the Hamlyn Publishing Group Limited
London · New York · Sydney · Toronto
Hamlyn House, Feltham, Middlesex, England.
Copyright © The Hamlyn Publishing Group Limited, 1973

ISBN 0 600 38018 1

Printed in Great Britain by Sir Joseph Causton and Sons Limited

INTRODUCTION

'King Steam, with his whistle and scream', was the supreme motive force behind the Industrial Revolution, the power that laid the foundations of our modern society. It was also the means by which man first realized his age-old dream of mechanised transport.

Although several factors–commercial pressures, biased legislation, and poor roads outside towns in the 19th Century–encouraged the development of the railway locomotive, road-going steam vehicles arrived earlier, and initially were much more promising.

Steam drove the first passenger vehicles, and it put new muscle into agriculture, so *Steam on the Road* goes into the rural byways as well as onto the highways–anywhere, in fact, except onto the iron road of the railway locomotive.

Steam seems outdated, supplanted by internal combustion, but present-day concern that world supplies of oil fuels may dry up suggests that there may yet be a future for the oldest form of power for self-propelled vehicles.

DBW

The publishers are grateful to the following organizations and individuals for the illustrations in this book: *Autocar*; H. J. Barker; Birthplace of Speed Association, Ormond Beach; British Leyland Motor Corporation; David Burgess Wise; Diana Burnett; J. I. Case Company; *Commercial Motor*; Pedr Davis; Mary Evans Picture Library; Fodens Limited; Henry Ford Museum; Hamlyn Group Archives; David Hodges; Jim Lee; Pete Lyons; The Mansell Collection; London Transport; Lucien Loreille, les Amateurs de l'Automobiles Anciennes; *Motor*; Musée Français de l'Automobile Henri Malartre; Musée de la Voiture de Compiègne; National Motor Museum, Beaulieu; Ron Reid; Science Museum, London; Nigel Snowdon; Kenneth H. Stauffer; Tate and Lyle Limited; Joseph L. Thomas, Secretary, the Sentinel Register; University of California, F. Hal Higgins Library of Agricultural Technology; University of Reading, Museum of English Rural Life; W. F. Warren; White Trucks. Most of the contemporary line drawings have been reproduced from manufacturers' catalogues.

NO OCCASION FOR HORSES
THE STEAM CARRIAGE BUILDERS

The Greeks may or may not have a word for it, but they certainly knew about the power of steam.

Around 1200 BC the philosopher Hero, who lived in Alexandria, Egypt, the intellectual centre of the Greek world, wrote about 'the expansive force of steam . . .', describing the cylinder, piston, slide valve and common clack-valve.

But Hero, and others like him, failed to put steam to any practical use. Instead, it was used to drive scientific toys, or as the basis for elaborate practical jokes; it is even claimed that some of the 'miracles' of the Egyptian magicians were worked by steam-power. Until the 17th Century, there was little practical advance in steam technology.

Then in the mid-1600s the second Marquis of Worcester took an interest in steam: his 'Water Commanding Engine' was said to be the first steam engine operated by a piston rising and falling in a cylinder. It is unlikely however, that the Marquis really understood how or why his engine worked. 'It appears,' wrote an early 19th Century commentator, 'that he injected cold water simply with a view to replenishing his boiler, and that he was not aware that it caused the condensation of the steam, or that this condensation was necessary in order to make the piston descend.'

In 1641, the Marquis visited Paris, and was shown round the Bicêtre lunatic asylum, where his attention was attracted by loud shouts from one of the cells. He was told that the inmate claimed he had made a great discovery, and had pestered the government so constantly for funds to perfect his invention that they had locked him away to rid themselves of an unwanted nuisance. The prisoner,

Solomon de Caus, claimed that 'people would travel faster by steam than the swiftest horses have ever been able to draw them.' The Marquis was unable to question the man further as his party was moved on; nor was his own project a financial success.

It was, however, improved on in the engines of Savery and Newcomen; this train of development was in turn brought to a relative pitch of perfection by James Watt's external condensing engine in the 1760s.

By then the first faltering attempts to move a vehicle by steam had already been taken.

Around 1681 Father Ferdinand Verbiest, a Jesuit missionary at the Chinese court at Pekin attempted to convert the Emperor by building a little steam carriage about two feet long which was driven by a jet of steam from the boiler impinging on a fan-bladed wheel geared to the rear axle; 50 years later another priest at Pekin, Father Grimaldi, copied Verbiest's design to amuse the Emperor Kang Hi.

Meanwhile, the Frenchman Denis Papin, inventor of the pressure-cooker—for which he had devised the safety-valve to control steam pressure—had experimented with the first model carriage driven by a piston engine, with transmission by ratchet wheels.

While he was in England in 1685, Papin had built 'a machine for raising water'. He regarded this use of steam as a 'mere trick', but resolved to discover some more positive application for this source of power.

In fact, his first engine, built in Germany around 1688, was also the first internal combustion engine, running on a mixture of gunpowder and air, but, finding this unsuccessful, he turned his attention to the steam engine.

This first appeared around 1690; by 1698, Papin wrote, 'As I felt there must be some other use for this discovery than pumping water, I made a little model waggon moved by this force, and it did . . . all I had expected of it . . . I think that the unevenness and twisting of the highway will make it very difficult to perfect this invention to drive carriages.'

A very significant development in the history of steam power, and in the history of transport, came in 1763. Nicolas-Joseph Cugnot, a native of Lorraine living in Brussels, built a model steam carriage which 'so much pleased Count Saxe that on his recommendation a full-sized engine was constructed at the cost of the French monarch.'

Capable of carrying four people, Cugnot's first full-sized steam-carriage was tested in 1769 in front of a number of dignitaries.

Writing in 1801, when Napoleon was taking an interest in steam traction, L. N. Rolland, commissioner-general of the artillery, reported: 'I have verified that it would have covered 1,800 to 2,000 toises (a toise was 6.4 ft) in an hour, had it not experienced setbacks'. But the capacity of the boiler was not equal to that of the pumps; it could not run for more than twelve or fifteen minutes at a time, and then it was necessary to let it stand for almost the same period to let the steam regain its original pressure. Moreover, the firebox was badly made and let the heat escape, and the boiler appeared too weak to withstand the effect of the steam under all circumstances.

'This test having indicated that a larger version of the machine could be a success, engineer Cugnot was ordered to supervise the construction of a new waggon . . . which was completed at the end of 1770 at a cost of 22,000 livres.'

This machine, which still survives, was a three-wheeled truck with a pear-shaped copper boiler ahead of the single front wheel, which had the twin cylinders astride it. Steam was admitted alternately into these cylinders through valves and exhausted at the base of the cylinder. A rocking beam linked the

Cugnot's *fardier* looks docile in this artist's 'reconstruction'.
In fact its directional stability was poor, which was hardly
surprising since the tiny tiller had to turn the mass of the
boiler and the engine as well as the front wheel. It was
involved in the first 'motoring accident'

two piston rods so that as one piston was pushed down, it pulled its neighbour up. The rods drove the front wheel through a ratchet mechanism.

The machine worked reasonably successfully, but directional stability was poor; on its first trial, 'a section of wall which got in its way was knocked down. That prevented further use being made of the machine.'

Over the next half-century, numerous experiments were made with small-scale models, but few full-size carriages were constructed. Even fewer were capable of actually moving.

In 1790, so it is said, Nathan Read drove a steam carriage through Warren, Massachusetts. This was the first vehicle to use a steering-wheel rather than a tiller. Around the same time, Dr Apollos Kinsey drove a steamer in Hartford, Connecticut.

Oliver Evans, having threatened to build a steam carriage since 1786, approached reality in July 1805, when his clumsy amphibious dredger *Orukter Amphibolos*, fitted with wheels for one journey, lumbered around Central Square, Philadelphia, and plopped into the River Schuykill, where its paddlewheel took over the somewhat unequal task of propulsion.

The first successful steam carriage was built in 1800 at Camborne, Cornwall, by Richard Trevithick, aided by his cousin and financier Andrew Vivian. Trevithick was one of the first engineers to use high-pressure steam and was also a pioneer of the double-acting engine, in which steam was admitted at each end of the stroke, so that the piston was moved both up and down in the cylinder by steam pressure.

On Christmas Eve 1801 Trevithick's engine puffed out of Camborne, was driven up the one in twenty slope of Beacon Hill, halted at the summit,

Trevithick's London Carriage of 1802 incorporated a primitive two speed transmission

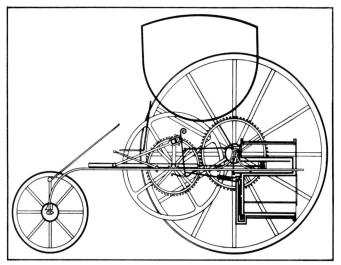

out of steam, and coasted back down to the town.

Four days later came a second trial. After driving a quarter of a mile, Trevithick and Vivian parked the carriage under a lean-to and adjourned to the local inn for a 'roast goose and proper drinks'. The carriage, left to its own devices, burned down the shed and cremated itself.

In 1802–3 Trevithick and Vivian built an improved carriage, which was shipped to London and fitted with a stagecoach body. From the coachworks in Leather Lane, Holborn, this was driven to Paddington, then to Islington and back to Holborn, the first prolonged journey by a self-propelled vehicle. During the run, it was involved in London's first motor accident, knocking down a section of garden railing.

Trevithick then abandoned road carriages in favour of railway engines; again he failed to pursue the idea to fruition.

The next attempt to construct a steam carriage was made, perhaps surprisingly, in Czechoslovakia. Josef Bozek, an engineer, built a little $\frac{1}{2}$ hp steam engine which he tried out in a carriage and in a paddle steamer; the carriage first appeared in Prague in September 1815. Bozek sat in front, a copper boiler at his feet, steering the vehicle with a tiller. Although the low power and limited boiler capacity of the engine meant that frequent stops were necessary, it ran well enough to encourage Bozek to persevere. In 1817 a public demonstration was organised in Prague's Stromvoka woods, watched by 'a numerous crowd'.

A collection was made, which Bozek hoped would clear the debts he had incurred in perfecting his engine. But a sudden thunderstorm sent the crowd scuttling for shelter, and in the confusion somebody stole the gate money!

Although the freemasons of Prague later gave Bozek 300 florins to pay his debts, he was obviously convinced that Providence was against his project, for he destroyed the carriage and two steamboats he had also built.

In 1819 the English inventor Medhurst built the first of two steam carriages. A single-seater capable of 5–7 mph, it ran between Paddington and Islington; rebuilt, it made the same journey two years later, watched by hundreds of passers-by. It was succeeded by a larger, four-seater version, which could cover seven miles in an hour without refuelling. Then family reasons caused Medhurst to abandon his experiments.

David Gordon invented some ludicrous machines, in 1827 proposing a carriage propelled by a midget railway engine running inside a huge wheel like a squirrel in a cage; while between 1824 and 1830 he experimented with four carriages propelled by articulated legs driven by two oscillating cylinders turning twin crankshafts. Slow, complex and destructive of the road surface, these carriages were a complete dead end in the development of the steam vehicle.

However, this period also witnessed a remarkable flowering in the building of steam carriages, led by British inventors.

So rapid was the progress of steam that horse owners felt their livelihood threatened – as early as 1825 an enthusiast for horse transport wrote an impassioned letter to the *Birmingham Gazette*, protesting against the growing use of steam on road and rail.

'In future,' he complained, 'the progress of our public vehicles will be traced, like that of some noxious reptile, by the dingy, dirty train they leave behind . . . Henceforth a flying chimney will alone mark the distant movement of the traveller, while the springing of an iron rattle, a profusion of black smoke, and a hissing as of many geese proclaim his near approach. I will not ask to enumerate *all* the miseries attendant on the proposed reign of darkness, soot and terror. I must, however, take leave to remind passengers by steam coaches of the certainty of their vapours – to request them to bear in mind that however fast they go horizontally they run the imminent risk of increasing in velocity tenfold, should any sudden freak of the boiler give them a perpendicular direction – and to warn the inhabitants of London against sending their accustomed present of oysters to their country friends by these conveyances, until they have first clearly ascertained that they like them stewed.'

One of the carriages which did most to influence the development of new designs, yet achieved no practical results itself, was the steam diligence designed by Julius Griffith and built in the Birmingham workshops of Joseph Bramah. It had a change-speed gear to give greater engine flexibility and a condenser to reconvert the exhaust steam into water, prolonging the intervals between refuelling stops – even 80 years later most steamers let their steam go to waste.

The carriage was too substantially built, however, and although its inventor worked on it for three or four years, its boiler was too small to generate enough steam to propel it. However, Bramah's workshops were a meeting place for many of the leading engineers of the day, and Griffith's carriage served as a touchstone to their powers of invention.

Like Griffith, many of the early builders of steam carriages tried to run before they could walk – almost before they could stand up.

For example, in 1824 Timothy Burstall and John Hill built a four-wheel-drive coach: it was so heavily constructed that trials at Leith and Edinburgh in 1826 and London in 1827 were disappointing. The boiler was too small, and exploded. A couple of years later Burstall and Hill came up with a two-

The Burstall and Hill steam coach, built in 1824, pioneered four-wheel-drive and front wheel brakes. The power unit was later adapted for railway use, with little success.

wheeled 'power pack' for converting ordinary stage coaches into steam carriages.

Then there was W. H. James, who, in collaboration with Sir James Anderson built a 'great diligence' with two boilers in 1826–8, which carried fifteen passengers through Epping Forest at 12–15 mph. An improved carriage with four boilers was tested in November 1829, but lack of finance caused James to abandon his experiments, although in 1832 he took out a patent for a carriage with a three-speed chain drive, with the ratios engaged by pedal.

One of the most outstanding of the early experimenters was a former surgeon from Cornwall named Goldsworthy Gurney, who also developed the limelight and central heating by radiators.

Gurney's first carriage of 1824–5 had articulated legs to push it along, but once the inventor saw the folly of this design he began work on a 3¾-ton carriage which featured an early form of servo-assisted steering—the driver's tiller acted on two small outrigger wheels which supplied the leverage to turn the main forecarriage to which they were linked.

Developing 14 hp, its twin cylinder engine had a voracious appetite for fuel, using about ten gallons of water and twenty pounds of coke for every mile covered.

However, it was with this vehicle in 1829 that Gurney undertook the first long-distance motor trip in history, from London to the fashionable spa city of Bath, a distance of 210 miles for the round trip.

The mechanism was poorly protected from road dirt and awkward to repair once it did break down. Though it was intended for a regular London-Bath service, it only made the journey once.

It did give horse owners cause for alarm, apparently, for passing through Melksham, where a fair was being held, the carriage was stoned by a crowd urged on by some coaching postilions, who feared redundancy if steam traction became common.

Two of Gurney's passengers were injured, and the travellers were forced to take shelter in a brewery, guarded by local constables. 'On the return journey the party timed their movements so as to pass through Melksham while the inhabitants were all safely in bed.' Although part of the driving mechanism had broken, Gurney reported that the last 84 miles from Melksham to Cranford Bridge, near Hounslow, were covered in 'ten hours including stoppages.'

Gurney was already working on a smaller, lighter

type of carriage, a drag or 'steam horse' to pull vehicles originally intended for horse draught. He was a man of some social standing: among the 'Persons of Distinction' who came to see and ride behind the drag were the Duke of Wellington and Robert Stevenson.

In 1830 three of these drags were bought by Sir Charles Dance, who used them to operate a passenger service between Cheltenham and Gloucester. The service made 396 journeys, carrying nearly 3,000 passengers, before opposition from local carriage owners, who rolled large stones in the path of the steamers (causing one of them to break its crank axle) plus a swingeing increase in the toll

Hancock's first steam carriage, named *Era*, was intended for a regular service between London and Greenwich, in 1833. Nothing came of this, but a second, more elegant, *Era* later worked between Paddington and Moorgate.

charges on the road, caused its withdrawal.

Subsequent attempts to operate Gurneys–again by Dance, in London in 1833, by Ward in Glasgow in 1831, and by Gurney himself, between Plymouth and Devonport as late as 1837–proved completely fruitless, and Gurney, having spent £30,000 of his personal fortune in trying to establish steam traction, returned to his other projects.

Gurney's contemporary Walter Hancock was more successful. His experiments began in 1824 with a three-wheeled carriage, at first using a curious power unit in which cylinders were replaced by rubberised bags which alternately expanded and contracted under steam pressure. Trials only proved the necessity of replacing this engine with a more conventional unit with oscillating cylinders of iron.

Hancock realised that at least half the troubles of contemporary steamers lay in poor boiler design: in 1827 he devised an ingenious form of boiler made up of embossed iron plates bolted and rivetted together which proved exceptionally efficient–fuel consumption was half that of Gurney's engine for a similar power output.

Hancock drove hundreds of miles in his little three-wheeler and in 1830 he built his second steam carriage, *Infant*. Its rear-mounted engine drove the back axle through a chain and sprockets, avoiding

The London & Paddington Steam Carriage Company ran a
regular service with Hancock's *Enterprise* of 1833, linking
Paddington with the Bank of England.

the troublesome crank axle which was a weak point
of other designs, such as the Gurneys.

Infant was a charabanc. Like all Hancock's subsequent designs it had a belt-driven blower to
quicken the fire, for its designer was one of the first
men to realise the importance of a forced draught
for improving the efficiency of a steam engine. He
also ran his boilers at a high pressure for the period –
70 psi was the normal safety valve blow-off setting,
although Hancock occasionally tried pressures as
high as 400 psi.

After trials *Infant* was modified to protect the
mechanism from dirt and dust, and in February
1831 it was used to inaugurate the first self-propelled
passenger service in London; in 1832 came a larger
vehicle, *Era*, followed the next year by *Enterprise* and
Autopsy.

On April 22 the London & Paddington Steam
Carriage Company put *Enterprise* into service between Paddington and the Bank of England. Although the service was an initial success, the
Company failed to pay Hancock what they owed

him, and, to make matters worse, their engineer,
Redmund, built a poor copy of *Enterprise*, and then
the company failed. Although Hancock recovered
Enterprise, he lost money in the deal.

In 1836, four Hancock carriages were put in
regular service in London, and a chain of service
stations was established. Over twenty weeks, 12,761
passengers were carried on 721 round trips from
Moorgate, over a total mileage of 4,200, at an
operating cost of 2*d* a mile. This was a most con-
vincing demonstration of the potential of steam
traction.

Most powerful of Hancock's carriages was *Auto-
maton*, a twenty-seat charabanc, capable of nearly
34 mph fully laden. On October 24, 1836 it was
driven from London to Epping, on the most uneven
main road out of London.

The following day the *Morning Herald* recorded
the journey:

'After remaining at Woodford for nearly a
quarter of an hour, Mr Hancock again started at a
rapid pace, and having ascended Buckhurst Hill at

the rate of at least seven and a half miles an hour, entered Epping amidst the loud cheers of some thousands who were collected in the town, it being market day, and created much astonishment among many of the country folk who had never seen such a vehicle before, and who could not imagine how it was moved without horses.'

Others were successfully building steam carriages at this time. There was Colonel Francis Macerone, an Anglo-Italian adventurer, who successively collaborated with and quarreled with both Gurney and John Squire, and was then ruined by a financier named Dasda, who took delivery of two Macerone steamers, which he passed off as his own invention to noble audiences in Paris and Brussels. Dasda sold his 'rights' in the invention for £16,000, but omitted to pay Macerone for the carriages. In 1841 Macerone tried to make a comeback, but again financial problems proved his downfall.

However, Macerone's carriages were obviously quite practicable. In a handwritten footnote to his autobiography, published in 1833, he exulted:

'Since the 7th instant we have been out every day, either to Harrow, Edgware or Watford, ascending Harrow, Stanmore & Clay hills at the rate of seven miles the hour.

'NB No Occasion for horses!'

Then there were Summers and Ogle, whose experimental carriage touched 35 mph on a journey to Southampton, and James Stone, who carried 36 people on his steam carriage.

However, vested interests were closing ranks against this new means of locomotion. The toll road owners heaped oppressive tolls on steam carriages—on the Liverpool-Prescot road, a steamer was charged £2 8s against 4s for a loaded stagecoach, while comparable figure on the Ashburnham and Totnes road were £2 and 3s.

In 1831 a Parliamentary Committee had reported that steam carriages were perfectly safe, did not damage the roads as much as horsed vehicles, were speedier and cheaper than carriages drawn by horses and that the excessive tolls should be reduced. But their recommendations were not adopted by Parliament, and by 1840 most steam carriage builders had given up the unequal struggle.

Meanwhile, a new line of development had been begun by the German engineer Jean-Christian Dietz and his sons Charles and Christian.

In 1832 Jean-Christian built his first 'remorquer', a three-wheeled tractor pulling a train of carriages which was tested between Brussels and Antwerp. He built two more tractors in 1835 and 1837; the last had eight independently-sprung supporting wheels and one central driving wheel.

Meanwhile, in 1834, Charles Dietz had established the first regular passenger service in Paris, using a tractor unit similar in design to his father's 1832 design.

It was greeted with rapturous applause by the French Academy of Industry. A reporter, Odolant Desnos, eulogised: 'This glorious coming of M. Dietz . . . afforded his passengers a spectacle as brilliant as it was novel. Words cannot describe the magnificent sight presented by the immense crowd which so covered the highway, from the park railings to the foot of the hill, that the carriage could scarcely clear itself a passage . . . it was for the able inventor the most magnificent of rewards.'

Christian Dietz built another remorquer in 1839, which in effect was a roadgoing railway locomotive, with eight wheels, of which six steered and two drove. Put in service in 1841 at Bordeaux, it aroused the enmity of the local waggoners, and on one occasion Christian Dietz had to beat off an attack with his poker.

Discouraged by their lack of commercial success, the Dietz family abandoned their road engines. But they had shown the way ahead to the traction engine.

The initiative in traction engine development passed to England, where stationary steam engines had for some time been mounted on wheels, to be drawn from place to place by horses to drive farm machinery.

In 1841, J. R. and A. Ransomes of Ipswich, Suffolk, introduced such a portable engine, equipped with a vertical boiler. This was designed by William Worby, whose grandson, William Worby Beaumont, was to write the 1900 Motoring classic *Motor Vehicles and Motors*.

The following year, the logical step was taken of linking the engine to one of the rear wheels by a chain. This enabled the machine to drag itself along; while a horse remained between the shafts at the front, it was used only to steer the engine.

Ransomes' next self-propelled engine followed locomotive practise more closely, and proved reasonably successful in service. It was built by E. B. Wilson of Leeds to the design of Robert Willis.

Already, however, these early road locomotives were exhibiting one major fault: they were too heavy for the roads of the day. Although it was claimed that steam carriages caused less damage to the road surface than horse drawn transport the problem of preventing self-moved vehicles sinking into the ground under their own weight had been a cause for concern for many years.

As early as 1771 Timothy Edgeworth had proposed a 'railway' which would automatically unroll beneath the wheels of a carriage and be taken up as it passed and several primitive forms of caterpillar

tracks were designed in the early 1800s. One of the best was conceived by Sir George Cayley, 'The Father of Aviation'. This featured transverse castor wheels so that the track could roll sideways to help steering. Cayley was friendly with Goldsworthy Gurney, and is reported to have owned a Gurney drag which he crashed into a shop front in London's Bond Street in November 1840, killing his engineer.

In 1808 the aptly-named John Dumbell patented substitution of 'Gothick or other kinds of arches, globes, semiglobes or segments' for ordinary carriage wheels to prevent them sinking on inferior roads or on bad ground.

While full size versions of the early caterpillar tracks were not produced, the Boydell plate, invented in 1839, provided a temporary practical solution to the problem of spreading the load on soft going.

Boydell plates were flat 'feet' hinged at a tangent to a large diameter wheel: the first application of these to a self-propelled vehicle seems to have been the traction engine built by Richard Bach of Birmingham to Boydell's own design.

Then, in 1856, two East Anglian companies which were to become familiar names in the traction engine world built Boydell engines. They were Burrell of Thetford, Norfolk, and Richard Garrett and Sons of Saxmundham, Suffolk; in 1857 William Tuxford and Sons built a three-wheeled Boydell engine.

This was the peak year of Boydell's invention, when the Endless Railway Company–shades of Timothy Edgeworth!–was formed to market it. Certainly the British Army was interested, for a factory at Woolwich Arsenal was building Boydell

'porte-rails', which were used on gun carriages in the Crimean War.

But the platypode progress of a Boydell-equipped traction engine was unreliable and noisy, the hinged joints wore quickly, and the system was abandoned.

A rival design, by William Bray of Folkestone, Kent, featured retractable spuds forced through slots in the wheel rim by an eccentric gear—it was obviously only suitable for agricultural use.

A much simpler idea was the fitting of cross-strakes to the driving wheels to increase adhesion—this was the system adopted by Thomas Aveling of Rochester, Kent, when he began experiments in 1858, converting portable engines into chain-driven traction engines.

Before long Aveling evolved what was to be the classic form of the traction engine—loco-boilered, with a steam-jacketed cylinder set on top of the boiler ('overmounted') behind the chimney, driving a crankshaft above the firebox.

Early models had a fifth wheel in front: this was used to steer the vehicle. Aveling's traction engine proved a success, and by 1862 forty were in service (some of the earlier engines were built for Aveling by Clayton and Shuttleworth).

Export markets were soon established: M. Tresca, sub-director of the Conservatoire Imperial des Arts et Métiers made trials with the Aveling *La Ville de Senlis* at Beaurain, while in 1868 another Aveling was towing an omnibus at Le Havre.

French manufacturers were not, however, entirely left behind by British developments.

In Nantes the engineer Lotz had begun experi-

Left: Lotz showed this cumbersome vertical-boilered three-wheeler and its omnibus trailer at the 1867 Exposition Universelle in Paris.

Below: at the opposite end of the scale, this curiously dainty little Virot tractor was built in 1884.

ments with steam engines in 1856, and his first traction engine, *L'Eclair*, took to the road in 1860. Four years later, he built a chain-driven engine with a steersman sitting in front of the chimney, which could haul loads of 3,500-6,000 kilogrammes at 8-12 kph. His 1866 *La France* was a real road locomotive – its boiler was so long that water tended to collect at either end when the engine was negotiating hills! Subsequent Lotz engines had the old-fashioned vertical boiler.

Nevertheless, *La France* was a powerful tractor, and on a 30.6 kilometre journey it pulled 29,353 kg (over 27 tons) at 7.3 kph.

Other leading French makes of the late 1850s were the Albaret from Liancourt, the Cail (built by a famous firm of locomotive engineers at Douai), the Gellerat, the Michaux and the curious Larmanjat, with an unusually short wheelbase.

Although the design of traction engines had become almost stereotyped by 1870, it seemed that there was always ample opportunity for flouting convention. Some makers followed the lead of Bray and Dubs in undermounting their cylinders, railway locomotive style – the 1862 Hornsby, Bonnel and Astbury had twin undermounted cylinders. Others, like John Fowler in 1871, built engines with three wheels, of which the best-known was *Progress* of the Cheadle Carrying Company. J. Taylor and Company of Birkenhead built the three-wheeled *Steam Elephant* which had two cylinders, a stubby boiler, rubber-cushioned wheel spokes and scaled six tons.

In 1879 Amédée Bollée *père* of Le Mans built two remarkable tractors, *Marie-Anne* and *Elizabeth*, which had engine/gearbox units foreshadowing the layout of the BLMC Mini. The gears lay below the crankshaft, making for a remarkably compact unit. The rear axle was driven by a shaft, and a power take-off to drive the wheels of a trailer was incorporated. Bollée's patent provided for all the wheels of a road train to be driven in this manner.

However, the Société Métallurgique de l'Ariège, for whom the tractors were built, failed to pay Bollée for them, and this most original line of development came to a dead end.

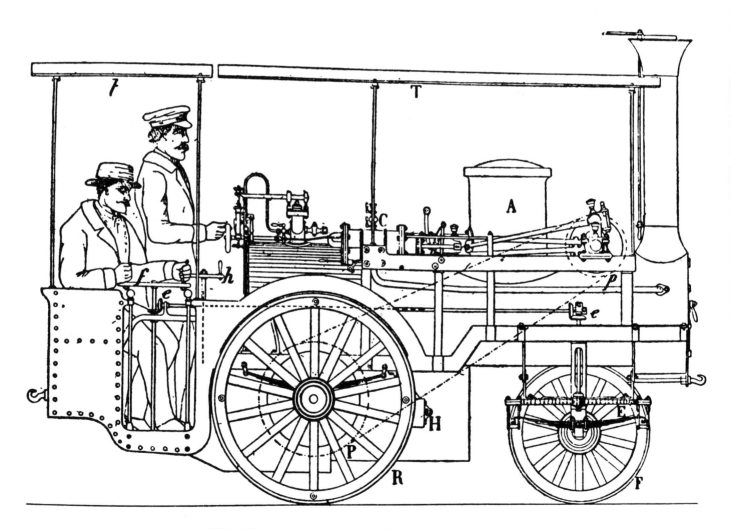

This Michaux road tractor of 1869–1870, with its chain drive and rear steersman, looked far more like a traditional traction engine than its contemporaries, such as the Lotz and Larmanjat.

Bollée's *Mancelle* of 1878 was the first vehicle to have a
vertical engine at the front, totally enclosed, with final
drive by propellor shaft and side chains; with the addition
of a gearbox, this layout was adopted in early petrol cars as
the *Système Panhard*. The twin-cylinder engine produced
about 10 hp and was mounted ahead of the front axle. Its
speed was controlled by the small concentric wheel within
the steering wheel. An outstanding feature of the *Mancelle*
design was the independent front suspension, with double
leaf springs. The stoker (chauffeur) stood on a platform at
the rear.

This particular *Mancelle*, which has a Victoria body, was
displayed as a veteran car at the 1900 Paris Exhibition. It is
now preserved at the Musée de la Voiture at Compiègne.

Ironic as it may seem, the anti-steam legislation that had begun in the 1830s actually favoured the development of the traction engine. The 1865 Locomotive Act laid down that: 'It shall not be lawful to drive any such Locomotive along any Turnpike Road or Public Highway, at a greater Speed than Four Miles an Hour, or through any City, Town or Village at a greater Speed than two miles an hour . . . at least three persons shall be employed to drive or conduct such Locomotive . . . one of such persons . . . shall procede such Locomotive on foot by not less than Sixty Yards, and shall carry a Red Flag constantly displayed.'

Obviously, it became no more than sensible for steam vehicle manufacturers to concentrate on the slower traction engines rather than the more glamorous steam carriages.

Although the requirement for the man walking in front to carry a red flag was repealed in 1878, the flag was still carried until the 1896 Locomotives on Highways Act raised the speed limit to 12 mph and did away with the peripatetic harbinger altogether.

In America the traction engine had made its first appearance around 1865. Design tended to be far less stereotyped than in England. For one thing, American engines had to be designed to burn cheap, locally obtainable fuels such as wood, straw and, later, oil, rather than the steam coal that fired British engines. Also, while skilled labour was cheaply available in Britain, it was at a premium in America. Consequently American traction engines lacked the finish of their British counterparts, and

were designed for ease of production. Spare parts were readily available, and easily fitted.

But whatever the differences between the products of the two countries, it was apparent that steam power was bringing new muscle to heavy haulage.

This chain-drive Aveling of 1862 was one of the first of its type to carry the cylinder at the front of the boiler, rather than above the firebox like a portable engine. The steersman sat in front of the smokebox and guided the engine with a tiller controlling the fifth wheel.

Following pages: Gurney's London–Bath Carriage of 1828 made the journey only once, and was plagued by breakdowns – at one stage a mechanical failure (probably of the cranked driving axle) occasioned the ignominy of having to call for horses to tow the vehicle.

MIGHTY ENGINES
STEAM REPLACES MUSCLE POWER

The first steam engines were simple, that is, the steam from the boiler was admitted to the cylinder, moved the piston and was exhausted to atmosphere, even though it still had some expansive power left. These engines were generally double-acting; at the appropriate points in the stroke a slide valve let steam in above and below the piston, so that unlike the petrol engine there were two power impulses per stroke.

It was apparent that an appreciable difference in power could be obtained by fitting a second, larger diameter, cylinder, designed to operate at a lower pressure and use the otherwise wasted exhaust steam from the high-pressure cylinder.

The two cylinders were designed to give identical power outputs, making for smoother running. Although the compound engine had been devised at the end of the 18th Century by Jonathan Hornblower, it was not used on vehicles until a century later.

A particularly neat form of compound was devised by Frederick Burrell, of Charles Burrell Ltd, in 1887. In this, the high-pressure cylinder was set diagonally above the low-pressure one. The pistons moved in unison, their rods acting together on a single-throw crank. Apart from increased power, economy and silence were the hallmarks of the compound engine. Some compounds featured 'simpling' gear, whereby the action of the valves could be modified to admit high-pressure steam into both cylinders simultaneously, to boost the torque when starting from rest.

To admit steam during the entire stroke gave the greatest power, but was wasteful of fuel and water, so the action of the valve was modified as required by a link motion.

When the engine was running light, the fore-and-aft motion of the slide valve was restricted by the linkage, so that steam was 'cut-off' early in the stroke, and then gave impetus to the piston by its expansive force rather than by boiler pressure.

The valve gear also enabled the engine to be reversed (this action could be used as a powerful brake). The most widely-used valve gear was the so-called 'Stephenson's link motion', invented in 1842 by William Howe, a fitter in Robert Stephenson's locomotive works; other popular valve gears were Joy's and Hackworth's.

To make the most of the engine output, British traction engines intended for agricultural work and short-distance haulage had two-speed gearing to the rear axle: road locomotives designed for long hauls used three-speed gearing. The engine had to be halted before a different ratio could be changed; when the driver wanted to run his engine as a stationary power unit, the gears were slid out of mesh.

American designers on the other hand did not believe in the multiple-speed transmission. Almost without exception their engines were large, powerful single speeders, with 'neutral' available by using a simple clutch.

It was not just in detail that American engines differed from the British product—layout and design were completely idiosyncratic, and American traction engines differed almost as widely from each other as from the British pattern.

Most American manufacturers used the locomotive boiler, although vertical boilers were quite common. Some makers, like Buffalo-Pitts, of Buffalo, New York, and Aultman of Canton, Ohio, used return-flue boilers, in which the main flue ran forward from the firebox the entire length of the boiler, then doubled back, on itself, with the chimney at the 'wrong' end of the boiler. This arrangement gave maximum draught, so that the engine could operate efficiently on low-grade fuels such as wood, straw, or corn stalks (particularly favoured in agricultural engines). Some makers offered alternative fireboxes, for coal, oil or wood and straw fuels.

Although these engines were more crudely and fussily finished than their British counterparts, they were far from lacking in ingenuity of design.

There was, for example, the 1885 Wood, Taber and Morse, built in Eaton, New York, which had four-wheel drive – a similar arrangement was used on the Lansing traction engine of the 1890s. In 1893 Charles H. Stratton of Moscow, Pennsylvania, produced 'an improved traction engine' with an undermounted cylinder, driving caterpillar tracks which 'enabled it to travel on the softest of ground.'

In Britain R. W. Thomson, the man who had invented the pneumatic tyre in 1845, designed an unorthodox vertical-boilered three-wheeled traction engine in the 1860s, for which he devised a special type of solid rubber tyre, loosely attached to the wheel rims, but free to 'creep' as the wheels revolved. These Thomson tyres 'immediately doubled the hauling power and allowed his engines to be run at speeds up to 10 miles an hour, whenever the Red Flag Act permitted it.'

To prove this, in 1869 a 6-ton Thomson was pitted against a 14-ton Tennant, another vertical-boilered three-wheeler. The Tennant was more powerful, and had more weight on the driving wheels, yet the smaller Thomson was its equal in pulling power, as both engines proved capable of drawing a load of thirty-four tons up a 1:25 gradient. However, Thomson's tyres were expensive – a set of three cost £241.

The original Thomson had undergone trials at Leith, in Scotland, in 1867, at the conclusion of which it had been shipped to Labuan, in the Dutch East Indies, where excellent results had been achieved in the carriage of goods and passengers.

A young officer in the Rifle Brigade stationed at Simla, India, R. E. B. Crompton, read of Thomson's work. Crompton had started work on a steam carriage – Blue Belle – while still at school at Harrow in 1860, when he was only sixteen years old.

Crompton made most of the parts of Blue Belle himself, casting and boring the cylinders for example, and contriving a differential inspired by spinning machinery in a Leeds mill. In India in 1866–67 he reconstructed Blue Belle with a professionally-built boiler, and used it as an inspection carriage. Many years later he recalled that 'she ran

Crompton's Blue Belle, in India during the 1860s. Parts of this machine survive, in the ownership of London's Science Museum.

a very considerable mileage, and on the whole worked very well. I was plagued by broken crankshafts, and my maximum speed was much cut down by the perpetual clinkering of the fire bars, caused by the only fuel available, consisting of briquettes made up of charcoal using cow dung as a binder'.

Crompton was *aide-de-camp* to the Commander-in-Chief, India, Sir William Mansfield, and often rode with the Viceroy, Lord Mayo. He persuaded Lord Mayo 'that the Indian Government would really be risking very little if it ordered one Thomson road-engine to experiment with.'

As a result, Crompton was appointed Superintendant of the Government Road Train, and a workshop was set up in Allighur, near Delhi, in 1870.

The first Thomson proved only a partial success, for it was designed to run on coal, and only wood was available. The results it achieved nevertheless showed that the programme was worthwhile. Crompton was sent to Edinburgh to discuss the design of four new engines suitable for drawing the heaviest loads then moved in India, like the 40-pounder Armstrong guns, which were at that time pulled by elephants.

Although Thomson was a bedridden invalid, he was far from idle. He had already redesigned his engines, and a larger version, called *The Advance,* was being built to War Office order by Robeys.

But Crompton was thinking in terms of 100 hp

Above: longest-lived of all the traction engine makers was Ramsomes of Ipswich, in production for a century, from 1842 to 1942. The firm's later products were marketed under the Ransomes, Simms and Jefferies banner, and many of these engines survive in the hands of steam enthusiasts, like this example seen in action at a 1969 rally.

Right: *Empress* is a 4 nominal horse power Garrett tractor, built in 1920 and originally used for haulage work in Suffolk. Tractors were light one-man operated engines built to take advantage of the Light Locomotive Act of 1903, which eased restrictions on road locomotives weighing less than 5 tons. *Empress* is a typical example – another is shown from a similar angle on page 91 – resembling a scaled-down traction engine of more familiar size. The tyres are bolted-on rubber strips.

engines, more than twice as powerful than previous designs. These were built to Thomson's design by Ransomes, Simms and Head, of Ipswich.

The first 100 hp engine, *Chenab,* was tested on Ipswich Racecourse in May 1871, when it was found that Thomson's 'pot' boiler was completely unsuitable for wood fuel, producing more sparks than steam. Its first major accomplishment was to set fire to the grandstand, which had to be rebuilt at Indian Government expense! An improved boiler designed by Lewis Olrick was subsequently fitted to *Chenab* and standardised on the other three Indian engines, the second of which, *Ravee,* was tested on a round trip from Ipswich to Edinburgh, towing a 103-seat omnibus trailer.

On the narrow and dangerous fen roads in the Isle of Ely the engine suffered its only mechanical breakdown when the brackish fen water with which Crompton had just filled the boiler caused some of the tubes to burst.

A major accident nearly occurred the following day when a Peterborough schoolmaster and amateur road engine builder named Montfort tried his hand at driving *Ravee*. All went smoothly for a while, but Montfort lost his nerve crossing a bridge, and it was only by snatching the steering wheel from him that Crompton prevented engine and trailer from plunging into the River Trent.

Crompton had a special permit from the Home Office which allowed him to ignore the Red Flag Act, and he made the most of this dispensation.

'Running parallel with the Great Northern Railway,' recorded Crompton, 'we overtook and passed goods trains. This constituted a record in road locomotion for that time. Though our loaded train weighed over forty tons, we were making speeds of well over twenty – probably nearer thirty – miles an hour.'

Just north of the Anglo-Scottish border, the engine pushed over a tollgate which an officious keeper refused to open, then proceeded to Edinburgh where Thomson was brought out in an invalid chair to watch the engine manoeuvring in the streets. The return journey to Ipswich was made without incident.

In India the four engines soon proved their worth. They were capable of hauling nineteen vehicles carrying a 40-ton payload at 5 mph up 1:18 gradients on the Grand Trunk Road. Not only were operating costs less than half those of animal traction, they were directly comparable with the best figures achieved by commercial vehicle operators in 1925.

In 1875 Crompton's contract ran out, and he returned to England, where his work was mainly to lie in the field of electrical engineering. Lord Mayo had been assassinated in the Andaman Islands, and as the other protagonists of the Government Road Train had either died or retired, a promising development was allowed to die of neglect.

Thomson steamers continued to be built for some years, as engine drivers appreciated their precise steering and excellent haulage capabilities; Robey's of Lincoln were still building the type in 1891, when they had completed more than fifty.

Among the devoted adherents of the Thomson engine were Harry Stanger, 'Instructor of the new corps of engine drivers at the Royal Arsenal, Woolwich', and Captain Lousada, manager of the Glasgow Tramways. But in Europe unorthodox

Right: war games – Fowlers on British army manoeuvres, circa 1900. The armoured B5 was one of four modified for supply column protection duties in the Boer War.

Below: this New Huber of 1903, built in Marion, Ohio, differed only in detail from the original New Huber of 1885. The company claimed that every one of the reverse flue engines they had built was still operating in 1903.

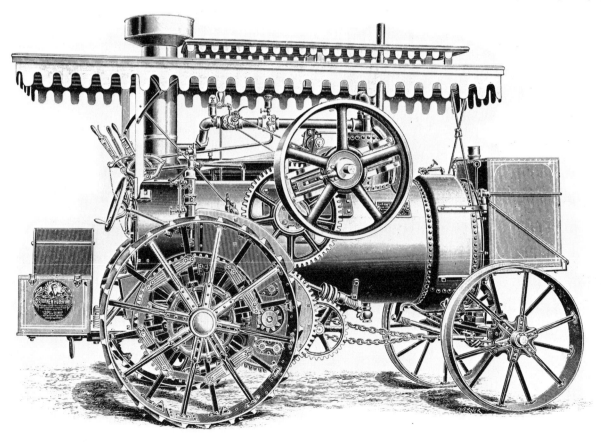

traction engine designs were fighting a losing battle against conventionality.

Conventional engines, indeed, had already shown their worth in battle, for the Germans had used two 20-ton Fowlers in the Franco-Prussian War of 1870, right up to the Siege of Paris.

Six years later, the Russians used 12 traction engines in their war against the Turks. The engines, which seem to have operated with complete success, were six Aveling and Porters, four Claytons and two Maltzefs (the latter were a rare breed, built in Briansk, Russia).

The most 'epoch-making' use of traction engines in warfare also marked the reappearance of R. E. B. Crompton in the field of steam transport.

In October 1899, Crompton had gone out to South Africa to command a detachment of three hundred electrical engineers which was to supply the electrical requirements of Lord Roberts's army in the South African War.

Traction engines were to be used to supply power to drive the dynamos which would operate arc-lights, searchlights and field telephones. Eventually, much to the disgust of Lord Kitchener, the engines were used to move and lay artillery – Kitchener even threatened Crompton with a court martial for bringing a gun into action outside Pretoria before the cavalry arrived, but only succeeded in making himself look ridiculous.

Crompton's engines contributed so much to army transportation that an Army Committee was set up with him on the board to further the development of mechanical transport for military transport. Ironically, the results of the trials organised by the Committee convincingly proved the superiority of the internal combustion engine.

In fact, this was just the first of many nails in the coffin of the traction engine. As soon as the type reached its peak, it began the long, slow process of dying.

Two of the many engines produced by Burrell at their Thetford, Norfolk, factory between 1856, when they built Boydell's first engine, and 1930, when the company became bankrupt. All were built to customers' individual requirements, and as with so many other makes this policy of non-standardization led to problems with maintenance when spares were required.

The best-known Burrell types, single-crank compounds, are illustrated here. The 1910 7 nominal horse power engine above is being driven with obvious determination at a rally in 1972 – or perhaps the driver's expression reflects frustration with a common single-crank problem, stalling when the engine is on dead centre?

Steam had been supreme in the Victorian era, but it needed trained men to use it to the best advantage. Internal combustion lacked many of steam's advantages, but it could be operated by anyone and was simple to maintain. As soon as the petrol engine became reliable, steam was fighting a losing rearguard action.

But there were still fields in which steam was supreme, like road making. The first steam road roller apparently appeared in 1859, in the guise of a Bray three-wheeled traction engine towing a separate roller. Soon, however, the archetypal steam roller with wide front and rear wheels or 'rolls' for flattening the road surface was developed. The front roll consisted of two wheels set closely side by side in a forked casting.

Best-known of the pioneers of the steam roller was Thomas Aveling of Rochester, who had tried pulling a 15-ton roller behind one of his traction

engines in 1865. Three years later he produced his first true steam-roller. Even these useful and slow-moving machines suffered under the 'Red Flag' Act, not least from the restriction that engines should be 'so constructed as to consume their own smoke'.

So Aveling decided to concentrate on export markets, where roadmen were less restricted by such legalities. Aveling introduced the road roller to the United States. Soon he was exporting half his output, and the rampant Kentish horse that was his trademark, together with the motto 'Invicta', was

Top: Aveling & Porter's vertical-boilered tandem roller was one of their rarer models. This example was still at work in Madrid in the 1960s.

Above: more typical of conventional steam roller design are the 1925 Wallis & Steevens and the 1926 Babcock & Wilcox.

Right: come into the garden . . . An Edwardian Fowler demonstrates that steering and braking on traction engines were not always as precise as they might have been. The saving factor in traction engine accidents was that they usually happened slowly.

seen literally all over the world. Of a total output of 12,700 Aveling and Porter steam vehicles, more than two-thirds were rollers, despite Thomas Aveling's nickname 'Father of the Traction Engine'.

Although other makers–Wallis and Steevens, Fowler, Garrett, Marshall, Robey, Burrell, Ruston and Proctor–built steam rollers, the Aveling machines monopolised the market, and outsold all the others.

British law-makers were convinced that sunlight twinkling on the moving crank and piston rods would cause restive horses to bolt, so road rollers–and many traction engines–had their motionwork concealed behind casings. For the same reason, the flywheel was almost always a solid cast disc. Where a spoked flywheel was used, as on early Wallis and Steevens engines, the spokes were concealed within a dished cover.

Many steam rollers were fitted with a scarifier, a

As long as road-surfacing merely consisted of flattening down stones of more or less even size scattered on the carriageway, the larger, heavier engines were in demand. However, after the First World War the emphasis changed as asphalt and concrete took over as road material.

On hot tarmac, the heavy conventional roller left dents in the road as it paused at the end of each forward and backward pass, so quick reversing was necessary.

Aveling's solution to this problem was a tandem roller, with full width rolls fore and aft. Its horizontal engine had twin cylinders and could be reversed without shutting off steam. The Aveling Tandem also featured a primitive form of power steering, a little three-cylinder engine controlled by a hand-wheel driving a worm-wheel acting on the steering quadrant of the front roll.

Another builder of tandem rollers was Robey of

toothed attachment which could be lowered to break up the old road surface so that the new dressing would be evenly laid down. It took manufacturers some time to cotton on to the obvious fact that the weight of the steam roller–especially on the larger 12-18 ton engines–was ample to force the tines of a scarifier through the road surface.

In the early days, before the roller arrived at the roadworks, 'a gaunt, scraggy engine suggesting the first attempt of an ancient Briton put in an appearance. To this was attached a kind of harrow with formidable iron teeth. This was the scarifier'.

Lincoln. Their tandem had a horizontal loco-type stayless boiler, feeding a quickly reversable double cylinder compound engine running on ball bearings. A fleet of 22 of these tandems was supplied to the Limmer and Trinidad Lake Asphalt Company in 1924, and a few years later the same company had three Robey tri-tandems built. These used twin rear rolls linked by a driving chain and were based on observations made by R. E. B. Crompton in the years before the First World War, when he was acting as engineer to the Road Board, and experimenting with different methods of road-surfacing.

Named after the famous horses bred by the Garrett family,
the Suffolk Punch of 1917–1920 was a light tractor with a
chassis and a rear-mounted boiler. Intended for agricultural
use, it was vainly hoped that this model would stem the
advancing tide of internal combustion engined tractors. This
is the sole surviving example of the eight which were built.

He reasoned that a roller with three rolls in tandem
would eliminate the wave-and-trough effect caused
by conventional rollers on hot tarmac. The Robey
tri-tandems proved quite effective, although prone
to frame fractures. Their working life continued
into the motorway era.

The best of the rollers designed for tarmac was
the Wallis and Steevens Advance, introduced at the
1924 Roads Exhibition. With wide rear rolls of
almost the same diameter as the front and positive
bevel steering, it had many of the best features of the
two-roll tandem. Its double-cylinder compound
engine gave instant reversing, and had no flywheel
to conserve inertia. The rear wheels automatically
adjusted to suit the road camber. Water, instead

of being carried outside the wheelbase in the
machine's tender, was stored in mid-mounted tanks,
keeping the weight between the rolls.

The Advance superseded existing tandem designs,
but the steam roller was under attack from the
motor roller, pioneered by Barford and Perkins of
Peterborough. In 1933 Aveling and Porter merged
with Barford and Perkins to form Aveling-Barford
and from then on the success of the motor roller was
assured. The last Aveling steam roller was built
early in 1948, but even now that the internal combustion engine has taken over, the company main-
tains its position as the world's largest manufacturer
of rollers.

But the working steam roller is not quite dead; a

32

handful are still cherished by some county councils – West Sussex is an example – who use them on road work in the summer.

Apart from road rollers, steam dominated the field of heavy haulage for many years.

By the Motor Car Act of 1903, road haulage engines were divided into two classes – heavy locomotives and light locomotives. The latter were restricted to a weight of 5 tons, and could only haul one trailer, but they were permitted to travel at 5 mph (heavy engines were restricted to 2 mph in towns and 4 mph in the country) and to be controlled by one man instead of two.

Often known as light motor tractors, these small traction engines were capable of an illegal 15 mph when the local police weren't looking, could travel between 12 and 30 miles without replenishing their water tanks.

One of the most famous of these steam motor tractors was the 3-ton Tasker 'Little Giant' *The Horse's Friend*, dating from 1903, which was originally purchased by an elderly lady to relieve the suffering of horses forced to pull laden waggons up Anerley Hill, near London's Crystal Palace. Acting as a mechanised trace-horse, this little engine helped over-burdened horses to the top of the hill for many years before returning to its makers for preservation. In 1969 it was auctioned for a record price of 4,400 guineas.

Other uses to which these smaller engines (the weight classification was raised to 7¼ tons in 1923) were admirably suited were furniture haulage, timber traction and general agricultural work.

Like most road-going traction engines, they used three-speed gearing (although the successful Garrett No 4 tractor of 1907-28 had only two speeds). Their light weight, and the high boiler pressure (around 200 psi) at which they operated made the single cylinder motor tractors quite skittish; the worm-and-chain gear controlling the centre-pivot steering was higher-geared than on other types of road locomotive to cope with this lively performance. Some early Wallis and Steevens compound steam tractors and a 1905 3-ton Garrett carried a spare water tank on the smokebox ahead of the chimney, presumably to counteract any tendency to rear up if power was let in too suddenly in low gear.

After the First World War, traction engines began to be fitted with solid rubber tyres, which became legally necessary in 1926. These gave extra resilience to the running of the engines – road locomotives were the only type of traction engine normally to incorporate road springing – and made extra speed possible.

But this development came too late, for the motor lorry had already progressed beyond the solid tyre and the pneumatic was rapidly becoming a commonplace.

The same fate befell the heavier road locomotives of over 5 tons, which were used in England right up to the late 1950s for hauling the heaviest loads, up to 90 tons or more using engines in tandem or triplicate. The heavy internal combustion engines built by companies like Scammell could deal with even greater loads – and move them more quickly.

An entirely different set of circumstances had led to the demise of the most spectacular road locomotive of all – the showman's engine.

The earliest showman's engines appeared in the

Below, left: this Fowler R3 compound engine was fitted with Botrail wheels, which were intended to improve traction on soft ground. In another attempt to improve adhesion, this 1877 Fowler (right) was fitted with 14 ft driving wheels, for service, apparently, in Scotland.

Following pages: *The Iron Maiden*, a 7 nominal horse power compound Fowler showman's engine was originally built for normal road use in 1920, and was converted for fairground use 12 years later. The flamboyant paint scheme is typical of this class of engine. It starred in the film 'The Iron Maiden'.

1880s, only 15 years after the stationary engine had first been applied to driving a fairground roundabout. Once the 'amusement contractors' had adopted the road locomotive as a means of hauling their sideshows and living vans from one fairground to another, it was not long before they impressed their colourful and flamboyant personalities on their engines.

With brilliant colour schemes, lavishly lined out, and gorgeously caparisoned with polished brass and copper ornamentation, these locomotives marked the peak of traction engine design. Brass stars were fixed on the motion covers and on the auxiliary belly-mounted water tanks, geometrical designs were painted on the flywheels, and cab covers were supported on 'olivers'–twisted brass columns in gingerbread profusion.

And not only was the showman's engine used for road haulage–once the fair was pitched on site it became a static generating plant, providing electricity to light the sideshows and rides. A dynamo

Moving pictures–Burrell 2281 *Queen of the Midlands* (above) on the road with Chipperfield's Bioscope near Chipping Norton, just before the First World War.
The Ransomes, Simms & Jefferies (below) of the early 1900s compares with the Ransomes, Simms & Head (inset) of the 1880s to show the progress–or lack of it–made in traction engine design over that period.

was mounted on an extension bracket projecting forward in front of the chimney and driven by a flat belt from the engine flywheel. At night the engine would form an impressive sight, as it stood gently pulsating with the driving belt slipping rhythmically over the pulleys, the battery of coloured lights beneath its canopy reflecting and twinkling on the polished brass.

Again, the production of the first generating plant suitable to be mounted on a traction engine was the work of R. E. B. Crompton, who in 1879 designed portable generators for Marshalls of Gainsborough. These first showman's engines supplied electricity to illuminate arc lamps, as the electric light bulb did not become a practical proposition until Edison's discovery of the carbon filament in 1880.

In July 1879 one of these Marshall-Crompton engines was used to illuminate Henley Regatta: 'the lighting effect on the river near the bridge was much talked of, and drew crowds to the river at night'. Crompton and his friends had to beat off high-spirited saboteurs with spanners on one occasion!

When the scenic railway became popular in the early 1920s, it was found that the starting load imposed by the fully laden cars was just too much for the dynamo, so a subsidiary booster dynamo known as the exciter was mounted behind the chimney; these 'special scenic' engines also had cranes fitted behind the cabs for lifting the scenic railway cars on and off the ride.

The showman's engine market in Britain was dominated by three makers—Burrell, Fowler and Foster. Burrell were the most prolific producers, building more than half the total output of showmans engines.

Although these are perhaps the more commonly recalled traction engines, in fact total output was not high—in the years 1885-1934, a total of eleven British firms built just 411 showman's engines. There were also some light showman's engines and a number of more or less worthy conversions of more mundane types. Some of these were contemporary modifications carried out by showmen; more recently, engines have been modified by 'enthusiasts' to increase their market value.

So much a part of fairground life for so long, the showman's engine declined quickly after 1939. The cause of its disappearance was the sudden availability of cheap ex-army heavy haulage vehicles and mobile generators; although the fairground proprietors have done their best with the gaudy paintwork, these mundane vehicles can never capture the majesty and sense of latent power that was the peculiar prerogative of the showman's road locomotive.

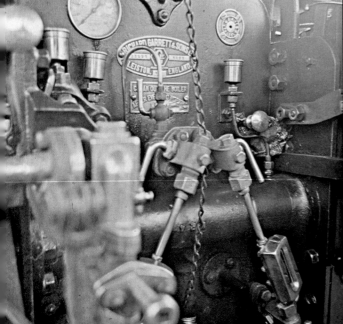

The first practical application of steam power to agriculture seems to have been the invention by William Bentall of a steam threshing outfit in 1806. Bentall, who was a leading agricultural implement maker, and had perfected the cast-iron plough in the 1790s, put his thresher into limited production. In the 1830s other firms introduced the first commercially available portable engines.

However, the real advantage that steam could offer, increased traction for ploughing purposes, was nullified by the great weight of the engines which, despite load-spreading devices like Boydell plates, were only too prone to become helplessly bogged down in the soft soil.

The answer came in 1850. John Fowler, a young Quaker and a locomotive engineer, was sent to Ireland on business at the height of the Potato Famine of the late 1840s, and he realised that the wholesale famine could have been avoided had the bogs been drained and capable of producing alternative crops to the potatoes that formed the basis of the Irish economy.

Fowler designed a ploughing system in which the traction engine stood still, gearing from the engine driving a drum under the boiler which pulled the plough across the field on a wire rope. Fowler's original 'mole-drainage' ploughing outfit was built for him by Ransomes of Ipswich and in 1850 it was used to drain Hainault Forest in Essex; the following year Fowler's engine was shown at the Great Exhibition in the Crystal Palace.

During the 1850s he persisted with the development of his ploughing engine; and his system was soon adapted for tilling the soil as well as drainage.

By 1858 a Fowler ploughing outfit could be purchased for £730; Ransomes turned out 20 of them that year, and Fowler had 40 sets of ploughing tackle on contract work.

In 1858, too, the Royal Agricultural Society of England awarded Fowler a £500 prize for his invention of the balance plough, which was an essential part of his system.

As perfected by the end of the 1850s, Fowler's system consisted of a powerful traction engine with a winding drum under the boiler, around which passed an endless wire rope, tensioned by two hinged clips. The wire was run across the field and round a pulley on a self-acting anchor on the opposite side. The anchor was a small truck mounted on four disc wheels which cut into the soil and ballasted on the outer edge so that it would not tilt over. The pulley could be engaged by gearing with a winding drum acting on a rope anchored well ahead of the truck. In this way the truck could be kept level with the traction engine as it moved forward at every return motion of the plough.

Fowler's balance plough unit was double-ended, with a seat and a set of plough-shares at each end. These were mounted at an angle on two wheels so that when one set of ploughs was in operation the other set pointed into the air. The haulage cable was kept off the ground by friction pulleys known as rope-porters, mounted on wheels so that the tautness of the rope kept them in line with the engine.

The entire action of the ploughing engine was virtually automatic, the whole apparatus moving forward after each return journey of the plough,

Top: this mid-Victorian oddity must have been the least practical ploughing engine ever devised, with its boiler threaded through the cable drum. The gentleman in the stovepipe hat looks quite confident that it will work, but his lugubrious engineer seems to be anticipating trouble.

Centre: far more businesslike, Fowler 8035 is typical of that firm's ploughing engines, with its belly-mounted cable drum. These engines could generate a pull of up to 50 tons on the cable.

Bottom: most steam ploughs were owned by cultivation contractors. This team of Fowlers, complete with ploughs and living van, is on the road between jobs, some time in the 1920s.

Following pages: the Geiser Manufacturing Company, of Waynesborough, Pennsylvania, was in business from 1875 until 1925. These Peerless engines, one with a spark arrester chimney used when wood or straw was the fuel, are typical of the firm's output.

The vertical-boilered Westinghouse of 1886 was built at Schenectady, New York, and was available with either horse or manual steering gear.

which could make from two to eight furrows at a time, depending upon the nature of the soil and the power of the engine.

If a portable engine was used instead of a traction engine, the system was modified to incorporate a separate winding drum in conjunction with two self-acting anchors, one at each side of the field, so that the rope followed a triangular course.

'To work Fowler's apparatus,' reported a mid-Victorian commentator, 'there are required one engine-driver, one ploughman, a stout lad to attend to the anchor, two boys to shift the rope-porters, and a horse and boy to supply the engine with fuel and water.'

The weekly wage bill for this team of six—including the upkeep of the horse and cart—totalled only £3 17s, of which the engine-driver took the largest cut, a munificent 18s.

John Fowler had demonstrated his steam-drainage plough system to the Royal Agricultural Society of Great Britain at Carlisle in 1855. Among the spectators was William Smith, a farmer from Bedfordshire, who realised the possibilities Fowler's invention had for agriculture, and put Fowler under contract to build him a windlass and other tilling apparatus. This was put into operation on Smith's farm at Woolston in the autumn of 1855.

Smith and Fowler did not remain collaborators for long as each had his own fixed ideas on the best way to utilise steam power in farming. The essential difference between them lay in the fact that Smith preferred the portable engine to the traction engine; he devised the 'roundabout' tillage system, on quite different lines to Fowler's 'direct' system.

In the roundabout, an ordinary portable thresh-ing engine drove a windlass with two drums, from which a wire rope stretched right round the area to be tilled, winding off one drum, and being re-wound on the other. To the rope was attached a powerful grubber, which broke up the soil to a depth of several inches. A second implement, the ridger and cultivator, was used to throw the soil into three-foot ridges.

Smith found that he was able to dispense with fallow fields, since the soil was broken up by rain and frost in the winter: he could grow abundant crops of wheat and beans in alternate years, at a cost of 8s 6d per acre. Since his farm was only 180 acres in area, these results proved convincingly that steam power was well within the reach of the small farmer.

The original roundabout apparatus was still in service 18 years later. Ploughing sets to Smith's design were marketed by J. and F. Howard of Bedford and later by Barford and Perkins of Peterborough. Probably the last roundabout outfit to remain in operation was an 1881 McLaren which was still working in East Kent in the early 1950s. In general, however, this system proved too clumsy to become widely adopted.

Fowler's early domination of the steam ploughing market was consolidated in 1860 when he established his own manufactory at Leeds. In the following year he introduced his 'double-engine' system, which became the standard method of steam cultivations, remaining unchanged in essence for over 70 years, until Fowlers built their last ploughing engine in 1932.

The engines were built as matched pairs, one for left-hand pull, one for right-hand pull, and would be stationed one at either side of the field. They took turns to pull the plough to and fro across the field.

The 1904 Baker, from Swanton, Ohio, was much more conventional in appearance than the Westinghouse or the engines opposite.

Top: a three-wheel Holt with a huge harvesting outfit on the American prairies. It was built by the firm which later pioneered and popularized the caterpillar track in the USA.

Centre: logging operations with a Best tractor in California in the 1890s.

Below: built for maximum traction on soft ground, this Best of the late 1880s featured ultra-wide rear wheels with chain 'grousers' to supplement the diagonal strakes.

Above: another pair of characteristic American engines, also from Waynesborough. These are Fricks (the company also used the name Eclipse). Their engines were in production from 1880 until 1921. Right: mixed line-up of British machines at a rally – rollers, traction engines and a Garrett converted to a showman's engine. The well-known rampant horse of Kent used by Avelings identifies their machines, nearest the camera.

The double-engine system was without equal for ploughing large fields – each engine carried 600 yards of cable – and, apart from its initial first cost, was economical in operation and easily transported from farm to farm.

Fowler did not live to see the fruition of his pioneering work: he was killed in a hunting accident in 1864, aged only 38. At the time of his death, his company was turning out half-a-dozen traction engines each week, and 300 Fowler plough-ing outfits were in use.

The coming of the internal combustion-engined tractor – especially the light, simple Fordson of 1917-on – really spelt the end of the ploughing engine. Even so, 40 years after the last Fowler ploughing engine had been built, some survivors were still in occasional use for heavy work, such as lake dredging, or hauling out tree roots. A couple, it is true, had suffered the indignity of having their steam engines replaced by 200 hp Sherman tank power units, but the steam plough is not quite extinct.

Very early on, John Fowler had established export markets for his engines, and it is recorded that Mark Twain commended the use of Fowler ploughing engines on the sugar plantations of the American Deep South to replace the slaves freed after the Civil War. But it was not long before the United States had established a traction engine industry second only to that of Britain.

Vast wheat and maize farms had been built up after the Civil War to feed the rapidly growing

population of America, swollen by the thousands of migrants from Europe. Harvesting was at first carried out by hand, or by horse power, using horses walking on endless conveyors that turned a flywheel from which drive could be taken by belt to power all kinds of agricultural machinery.

By 1880 the primitive horse-steer traction engine had made its appearance: within a couple of years the self-steering engine was firmly established, one of the earliest of this pattern being the Hooven, Owens and Rentschler *Monarch* which took first prize at the great St Louis Fair of 1881.

Although the makers of the Monarch guaranteed 'satisfaction in every case', there were still reactionary fuddy-duddies around.

Westinghouse, in their 1886 catalogue describing their new range of belt-drive vertical-boilered traction engines, primly observed: 'a *steering apparatus* may also be applied to any engine, although we do not recommend its use while running upon public highways. It is better and safer to depend upon a team to guide'.

However, when the 15 hp Westinghouse was adapted for drawing a plough, it had ordinary wheel steering. An auxiliary water tank was mounted above the front axle, and may have had something to do with helping adhesion on the front wheels. Interestingly enough, the indigenous American manufacturers preferred direct haulage ploughing engines, and only a couple, like Kelly and Russell (both Ohio makes), went in for cable ploughing.

Top: built by the Oneida Iron Works, this American engine of 1880 had chain drive but was steered by a horse harnessed to the front axle.

Above: advanced design–this 1925 engine had a fan-cooled condensor and automatic self-feed coke stoker. It was built by the A.D. Baker Company of Swanton, Ohio.

Below: equipped for horse or wheel steering, this 1885 Case burnt straw as fuel.

Probably the most spectacular of the American direct-draught ploughing engines was the Best, built for use on the Pacific coast, where single fields could cover an area of 20,000 acres.

Daniel Best of San Leandro, Alameda County, California, had been a manufacturer of agricultural machinery for twenty years before he developed his steam harvesting outfit in 1889. Best's massive three-wheeled engine was based on the 1888 design of D. L. Remington of Oregon. It weighed 11 tons with a full water-tank and could turn in a 16 foot circle, thanks to 'ingenious and effective steering apparatus'.

Its twin-cylinder engine developed 40 bhp with 100 psi boiler pressure and 60 bhp with 150 psi pressure, and 'this power was believed to be multiplied 25 times by means of its application to the rims of the driving wheels instead of centrally to the axle'.

Be that as it may be–and it probably wasn't–the Best combine harvester was an impressive sight, standing over 20 ft high, running on 9 ft diameter driving wheels, and capable of cutting a swathe 42 ft wide through standing corn. It travelled from farm to farm in a lengthy convoy incorporating engine, thresher, header, watertank wagon and cookhouse.

Operated by eight men, the outfit–which supplied steam to the combine harvester through flexible pipes from the boiler–could cut, thresh, reclean and sack between 65-125 acres of grain a day. Burning the waste stalks of the grain, the Best was extremely economical to run.

Perhaps the ultimate Best was the 41-tonner operated around the turn of the century by the Middle River Farming Company of Stockton, California, for harvesting, ploughing and planting on soft peat soils. It was prevented from bogging down by 15 ft wide, 9 ft diameter driving wheels supported by outrigger derricks.

Most prominent of the American traction engine makers was the J. I. Case Threshing Machine Company of Racine, Wisconsin. They had built their first agricultural steam engine, a portable, in 1869–it had the unusual feature of wood-spoked wheels but was otherwise conventional. Case built their first traction engine around 1880, and after trying various patterns–horse-steered and return flue layouts–they settled on the overmounted loco-boilered pattern that was to remain their staple layout until the end of traction engine production in 1925.

Their 1907 25 hp engine featured a Woolf compound power unit, with the high-pressure cylinder mounted in tandem with the low-pressure cylinder. This gave certain advantages–only one

set of valve gear and one crank were needed—but it also gave the major disadvantage that the engine could be stalled on its dead centres. The engine had only one forward speed, and drove through a friction clutch inside the flywheel rim (these features were common to many American makes but rarely found outside that continent).

Throughout North America traction engines like the big Best machines hauled impressive loads in logging operations, tending to be more extensively used in dry regions like California than in the wetter forests further north, in Oregon for example.

Other leading American makes were the Huber,

Foster of Lincoln were one of the last firms to build a traction engine—like Ransomes, another contender for the title, their final engine left the works during the Second World War. The *Little Gem* (left), which was first registered in 1934, demonstrates threshing at a rally in 1970.

Below: another model from that prolific American manufacturer, the J.I. Case Company of Racine, Wisconsin. This is an 1886 engine.

with a reverse-flue boiler and engine over the firebox, 'which won each of the four great traction engine contests at the World's Fair at Chicago, in 1893', and the Gaar-Scott, whose 1906 models rejoiced in the names of 'Old King Coal' and 'Strawburner King'. Gaar-Scott's threshing machine was known as the 'Harvest Queen'; 'If you couple this Harvest Queen to a Gaar-Scott King Coal', ran their advertising, 'you will be the jolliest soul in the field. Are you ready for the music to begin?'

But the music had nearly run down, even in 1906.

America was the first country to make extensive use of the internal-combustion-engined tractor, and the vast dinosaurs of steam were doomed to extinction. By the 1920s, the American traction engine was almost dead.

However, other countries than England and America had played a part in the rise and fall of the agricultural traction engine.

There had been the French makers who followed in the wheel-tracks of Lotz—Albaret of Rantigny and Liancourt, who built traction engines and rollers from 1880 to 1922, L. and A. Pecard Freres of Nevers, active from 1900 to 1929 and La Societé Française Vierzon (1915-31).

From Canada had come the Waterous (1890-1920) and the White, and from Poznan, Poland, the Cegielski, built during the five years from 1915.

The Austro-Hungarian Empire produced several types of traction engine—there was the Hoffherr and Schrantz, built in factories at Vienna and Budapest between 1902 and 1930, mostly to the British

50

Clayton and Shuttleworth design, although some shaft-and-bevel driven models were produced; also from Budapest came the Elso-Magyar Gazdasgi Gepgyar (1911-30) and the International (1915-27).

The unlikely spectacle of steam in a cold climate was provided by the Swedish Munktells Mekaniskiska Verkstad Aktiebolag of Eskilstuna, who began production in 1890 with a chain-driven engine which had the cylinder above the firebox, but by 1900 were building engines which followed the English pattern more closely.

However, the longest and most positive contribution to traction engine history after the two major manufacturing countries had been made in Germany.

First on the scene had been the famous locomotive engineers J. A. Maffei AG of Munich, who built an undertype traction engine on railway locomotive lines as early as 1860; the engines were in production until 1927, although whether output was continuous is uncertain.

Although only in existence from 1912 to 1918, J. Kemna, of Breslau, built the most powerful traction engines ever made – massive ploughing engines of 230-310 hp, with a cable drum under the boiler, looking very much like a stretched Fowler.

But when the last traction engine of all was built, in 1942, it was appropriately, a Ransomes. The British company which had produced the first traction engine of all had also written the final word, after a century of continuous production.

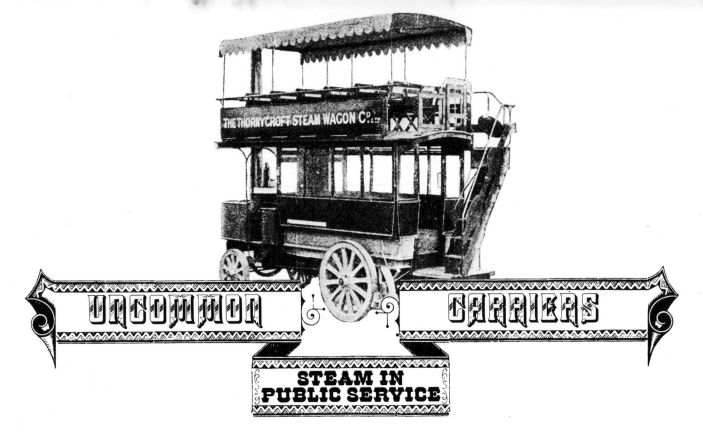

UNCOMMON CARRIERS

STEAM IN PUBLIC SERVICE

Although Thomas Hancock and Sir Charles Dance had proved the practicability of public steam omnibus services in the 1830s, the revival of the motor vehicle saw few attempts at operating steam-powered buses.

Harry Lawson, self-appointed 'Father of the British Motor Industry', proposed to put a fleet of 200 De Dion-Bouton steam double-deckers into service in London in 1898. However, this proved to be another of Lawson's schemes for parting credulous investors from their money, and although £50,000 was raised, only a couple of the buses saw even experimental use.

Between 1899-1905, a handful of British manufacturers—Lifu, Leyland, Straker-Squire, Thornycroft—built steam buses, and some of these saw limited service. Without exception they proved uneconomical, and it was left to one man, Thomas Clarkson of Chelmsford, Essex, to prove the viability of steam for public transport.

Clarkson's works had built over eighty buses in the period 1902-08, but eventually the various bus operators closed their ranks against the steam bus, most of them standardising on the successful petrol chassis such as the Milnes-Daimler.

Acting on the well-tried theory 'if you can't beat them, join them', Clarkson founded his own bus company, the National, in 1909 (the new company also took over the Chelmsford factory). By the beginning of 1914, the National Steam Car Company had 173 buses running in London; Clarksons were also in service in Torquay and Harrogate.

But as well as being his own best customer, Thomas Clarkson was his own worst enemy, for he steadfastly refused to standardise his designs, so that virtually every Clarkson steam bus built differed to a greater or lesser degree from the other buses of his National fleet.

This obviously made the cost of maintenance extremely high. Then drivers became hard to find, especially in the summer, when the heat from the underbonnet boiler could become unbearable, and the green and white National Clarksons were withdrawn from service in 1919-20.

A privately owned steam bus service which had been operating in Ryde, on the Isle of Wight, since 1909, using a Clarkson, an elderly Gardner-Serpollet and five slightly younger Darracq-Serpollets originally imported from France for the Metropolitan Steam Omnibus Company, disappeared around the same time, as did a solitary Yorkshire steam bus operated by Grimsby Tramways.

This marked the end of the steam bus in regular service, even though the Clarksons had achieved a remarkable reputation for reliability on the road.

The Sentinel, Mann and Foden companies all experimented with one-off steam buses in the 1920s. Foden's *Puffing Billy* was used to carry the famous Foden Works Band, and a replica of this vehicle, the last steam bus to be constructed anywhere, was built in the late 1960s by a Norfolk enthusiast, G. E. Milligen, on a vintage Foden wagon chassis.

During the late 1930s the German Henschel company constructed a number of steam buses and trucks to the design of the American Abner Doble, on the premise that use of the steam engine would make Germany independent of imported petrol, as cheap home-produced fuels could be used.

Opposite: a Thornycroft steam bus of 1902, used by the London Road Car Company.

Above: the Gillett Motor Company of Hounslow were in business from 1897 until 1901; they built this bus in 1898 for the Thames Valley service operated by the Motor Omnibus Syndicate of London.

Above: *Puffing Billy*, a replica of the Foden Works Band's steam bus, was built on a Foden wagon chassis in the 1960s.

Below: one of the first self-propelled vehicles to be seen in Japan, this 1905 White bus made the 6½-mile journey between Osaka and Sakai eight times a day.

Foden steam wagons of the mid-1920s (above and right) differed little from their pre-war counterparts, although the chain-operated centre-pivot steering of the earlier models was replaced by Ackermann-type axles. An increase in overall length gave only marginal improvement in payload, and Foden eventually changed to an undertype engine layout. The wagon above has a three-way tipping body.

Although the Doble-Henschels developed 120 bhp and were claimed to accelerate and cruise faster than comparable petrol-engined vehicles, production remained small, and Henschel's military vehicles built during the Second World War featured conventional internal combustion power units.

But if the steam bus was short-lived, the steam tram was positively ephemeral. Used in the period of transition from horse to electric haulage, the steam tram engine (which was a haulage engine pure and simple, trailing the 'dummy' passenger car) was even more hedged round by restrictions than the traction engine. Not only had the motion and wheels to be enclosed virtually to ground level, but no smoke or steam was to be emitted. Every precaution was taken to prevent the hapless pedestrian from being wound into the works or the restive horse from being frightened by flashing cranks and coupling rods, with the inevitable result that the steam tram became a somewhat characterless machine, with few noticing, let alone mourning, its demise.

However, in 1876 a Californian, S. R. Matthewson, devised a splendidly lunatic steam tram engine with the front end shaped like a horse (with a bell

between the ears!) and a 5 hp steam engine 'accommodated in the imitation horse's rump!' The driving cab resembled a rococo telephone booth; it was claimed that the unlikely contraption could travel at a breakneck 8 mph and pull up 'within a space of 20 feet'.

After the turn of the century the steam tram was used only spasmodically on rural light railways. These were operated on meagre shoestrings; which meant that the slightly scruffy condition in which the engines and rolling-stock were maintained only helped them in living down to their image.

But if the steam tram was a comparative failure, the steam wagon dominated heavy haulage in Britain in the formative years of the motor age. Though steam wagons were built and operated in other countries, Britain led the way, and persevered longest with the development of the type.

Few of the mid-Victorian experimenters bothered with the steam wagon; in many cases it was all they could do to persuade their vehicles to move with just a driver aboard, without bothering about any additional payload.

Brown and May, steam engineers of Devizes, Wiltshire, are recorded as having built a steam van in 1875; doubtless it was based on the company's

traction engines, but had a vertical boiler.

Nine years later, James Sumner, a young steam enthusiast from Leyland, Lancashire, produced a steam wagon of his own design, a 5-tonner, built to carry coal from the local pits to Stanning's Bleach-works at Leyland. It was not an outstanding success, and Stanning was penalised for his support of the steam wagon. When he stood at the first local County Council election, he was defeated by Boothman, the Liberal candidate, on the sole grounds that his 'traction engine' was breaking up the local roads and bridges.

The wagon's last journey was the fifteen-mile run from Leyland to Ormskirk, with William, James Sumner's younger brother, acting as 'red flag boy and general assistant in a host of major troubles'.

The journey took from Friday morning to Monday evening, and included a session in court answering a police summons for leaving the wagon broken down and unattended on Saturday night.

When they returned to Leyland the wagon was put into immediate and permanent retirement, and its engine used to drive the local sawmill.

Sumner then built a light twin-cylinder engine which he fitted in a second-hand tricycle, which proved to be so speedy that it attracted unwelcome attention from the police.

In 1892 Sumner inherited the family business, which had grown from a village smithy at the time of the Napoleonic Wars to a fully equipped engin-eering works capable of producing iron castings up to half a ton in weight and brass castings up to half a hundredweight. With it he also inherited a load of debts, and to clear these, Sumner adapted his tri-cycle engine to drive a lawnmower. Rugby School bought the first of these, and was followed by many schools, institutions and sporting organisations.

During one sales demonstration the control of a steam lawnmower was entrusted to a gardner: he opened the throttle too wide, and the machine

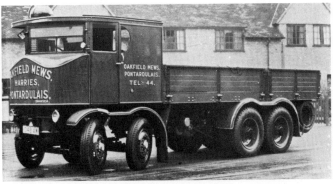

Left, top and centre:
early Leyland Lancashire steam
wagons in service in the early 1900s. Using a steamer to
shift coal seems eminently sensible, but the driver with a
load of matches and a hood neatly set to catch sparks from
the chimney is all set to go out in a blaze of glory.

Left, below: the
transverse-boilered Yorkshire wagon from
Hunslet, Leeds–this is a 1904 5-ton model–offered
mechanical accessibility coupled with a
good carrying capacity.

Above: both ends of the Sentinel scale–
an early Glasgow-built 'Standard' of 1912 vintage and the
technically-advanced DG8 of 1930. Eight examples of this
model, which featured the eight-wheel steering devised by
Sentinel, were built and this one, 8130,
was the last of them.

Below: another make from Hunslet was the Mann Steam
Cart; this 5-tonner was exhibited at London's Agricultural
Hall in 1903

ran away from him, despite his frantic cries of 'Whoa!', and trundled with a mighty splash straight into an ornamental lake.

The relaxation of the law relating to motor vehicles in 1896 gave Sumner the chance to build something more exciting than lawnmowers: the Lancashire Steam Motor Company was formed, with Sumner and Henry Spurrier Junior as the guiding spirits.

Before 1896 was out their first steam wagon was running. A 30 cwt van, it had a vertical oil-fired boiler and a two-cylinder compound engine developing 10-14 hp, driving the rear axle through a three-speed gear with friction clutches. A three-ton truck followed. Both vehicles did well in the commercial vehicle trials of the day, and carried off many awards. The truck was eventually sold to Fox Brothers of Wellington, Somerset, who used it to carry wool between mills within a radius of nine miles. As a result of their experience, it was decided to replace the oil firing by coal.

Progress was–relatively–rapid; a new factory was opened in 1902, and by the end of the following year 39 steam wagons were in service, including the first fleet of Leyland vehicles, operated by the Road Carrying Company of Liverpool. Three mail vans had been exported to Ceylon in 1901.

In 1904, 33 Leylands were built by the 160 employees of the company, and already London boroughs were beginning to use these steamers and the similar Thorneycroft for municipal service. Chiswick had bought a Thornycroft tipping wagon in 1897, and Chelsea and Wandsworth were building up fleets of Leylands with interchangeable street watering cart and tipping dust cart bodies. Even though Leyland were to continue to produce their steam lorries for some years to come, the writing was on the wall from the moment that they introduced the Pig, their first internal combustion engined wagon, in 1904. It was a failure, but the company persisted with the development of

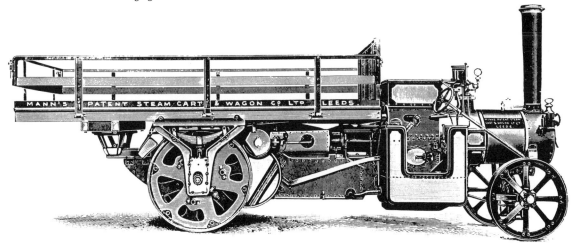

petrol lorries, and by 1910, they were able to point out that as 'the only builders of steam and petrol wagons, their advice was unbiassed'.

'For loads below four tons, petrol is most suitable. For loads between four and six tons, the advantage may be either way, but for heavy loads, above six tons, with a mileage of forty or less per day, there is no doubt that steam is the more economical source of power at the present price of petrol and rubber.'

It seems, however, that many of those early vertical-boilered wagons were inefficient steamers – the notable exception being Alley and MacLellan's 1906 Sentinel – originally built in Glasgow, then from 1915 at Shrewsbury, which its makers accurately described as, 'massive and durable . . . simple and solid'.

Certainly, out of the commercial vehicle trials organised by the Liverpool Self-Propelled Traffic Association between 1898-1901 and the War Office in 1901, there emerged a distinct type of steam

wagon that was peculiarly British, and dominated the market for a quarter of a century – the overtype.

It had traction-engine type motion-work mounted on top of a short locomotive-type boiler; the earliest examples, appearing in 1901, were produced by Mann of Leeds and Foden. Many separate makes of overtype subsequently appeared, including Burrell, Clayton, Foster, Garrett, Robey and Wallis and Steevens, but Foden never relinquished the lead they had taken in 1901. However, the overtype had one major ineradicable drawback – the length of its boiler and cab greatly impaired the carrying capacity unless an excessively long wheelbase was used. And in the increasingly load-conscious 1920s this proved a fatal drawback. The vertical boilered undertype, which only Sentinel had consistently produced (although Yorkshire had turned out a fair number of their transverse-boilered undertype, which shared the advantages) was to dominate the later years of the steam lorry.

Opposite: the Super-Sentinel was current from 1923 until 1930. Production models had solid tyres but many, like this example which is a familiar sight at British rallies, were subsequently converted to pneumatics. The engine is slung beneath the chassis, making possible a much larger payload platform than was possible with overtype engines (see page 54). Final drive is by chains, and steam brakes on the rear wheels were another feature of the design. The enclosed cab was normal on these wagons; as here the windscreen was frequently left open for ventilation.

Above: no progressive estate was complete at the turn of the century without a Leyland steam lawn mower. Similar devices were available in America.

Right: America's first light steam commercial vehicle was the 1900 White van, although the White Sewing Machine Company had earlier built an unsuccessful 5-ton truck.

Sentinel's original design was sound enough to keep the company going until 1923–by 1920 production was running at 32 a week–and then the company consolidated its lead in the undertype field with the Super-Sentinel, which had a very compact twin-cylinder engine incorporating a neat differential gear in the crankshaft. But the Sentinel was only a single-speeder, and could not be operated as efficiently as the multi-geared wagons.

In 1927 came the DG (double-gear) two-speeder, with a gearbox/differential in unit with the engine. Simultaneously came a six-wheeled Sentinel, one of the earliest rigid steam six-wheelers (Garrett were first, in 1926, Sentinel and Foden only just behind).

Sentinel quoted Longfellow to describe the DG6: 'built for freight and yet for speed . . . a beautiful and gallant craft'.

Their copywriter kept up the image: 'This modern clipper of the roads makes light of its heavy freights and glides from port to port with a speed and safety only its 120 hp engine and sixteen-shoe steam-aided brakes can impart.

'At all times master of its work, certainty of trouble-free operation and lowest running costs follow in its wake.'

A further breakthrough came in 1930 with the DG8, in which the front four wheels steered and the rear four drove.

The ultimate Sentinel appeared in 1933, the model S, with a four-cylinder single-acting engine. Unlike earlier Sentinels, this one was mounted on pneumatic tyres as standard (a clever feature of the design was a steam-driven tyre pump).

Other makers built undertypes–Clayton, early on the scene in 1927 with front wheel brakes and Atkinson, whose wagon used a 'uniflow' engine, with steam admitted at the top of the stroke and exhausted through ports in the cylinder walls at the bottom of the stroke, while Clarkson's swan-song was the 1921 X-Type, with a V-twin engine and three-speed gearbox. Five years of development were behind this model, and control was as simple as a petrol lorry.

'Can you Afford to do your Transport in the Old Way?' asked Clarkson: people, it seemed, could, and the company passed from the scene.

But of all the undertypes, the most famous of the Sentinel's challengers was Foden's splendid Speed Six and Speed Twelve range. The Speed Six, named after E. R. Foden's beloved Bentley, appeared in 1929. With a 90 bhp engine, and mounted on pneumatic tyres, the Speed Six was reputed to be good for 60 mph, or three times the existing legal speed limit.

But only a couple of years later Fodens turned to the diesel engine, abandoning steam for good.

A major reason why the steam wagon had survived so long in Britain was that, while petrol was

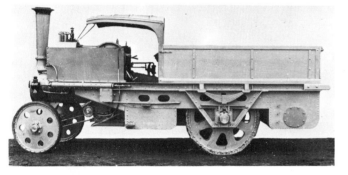

Two stages in
the development of the Foden steam wagon–
the 1900 3-tonner (left) which took part in the War office Trials of that year and (below) a 1912 4-tonner. Both show clearly that a disproportionate amount of the overall length was taken up with boiler and engine.

taxed relatively heavily, the coal burned by steamers was not, making steam lorries far cheaper to run.

In an effort to equalise the situation, the 1933 Road Traffic Act introduced a differential system of taxation for commercials, trebling the annual licence fee for steamers. Duties on diesel-engined vehicles were lighter, and on petrol commercials lightest of all. The Act made the running costs of the three types of vehicle approximately equal, but the operators did not see it that way, as there was suddenly no financial inducement to put up with the disadvantages of the contemporary steam wagons–the poor forward vision, the hot cabs, the inadequate brakes.

Sentinel tried to readjust the situation by persuading the top American steam engineer Abner Doble to come to Shrewsbury to develop a revolutionary new type of steam motor lorry.

The Sentinel-Doble generated high pressure steam in an efficient flash boiler, initially coke-fired and later oil-fired. It is reported that the lorry attracted an unusual number of speeding summonses; it could go, so the test drivers claimed, faster than it could be steered, and cover 540 miles in a day, including loading and unloading.

But only two prototypes were built, and never became a commercial proposition. Sentinel continued production of the S model until 1950, when 100 were shipped to the Argentine, with boilers modified to burn the cheap local brown coal, and a solitary Sentinel went to the Welsh Coal Board.

After that Sentinel went over to production of rather ugly diesel trucks, but the heart had gone out of the company, and seven years after the last steam waggon–Sentinels always spelt it with two 'g's–had left Shrewsbury, production of the oilers finished also, and the most successful marque of steam lorry became just a memory.

Above: Controls of the last of the Sentinel steam waggons, the 1950 model, of which 101 were built (this one stayed in Britain). The Foden Flexible Six Steam Waggon of 1920 (below) was one of the first articulated vehicles, and had a 10-ton payload. Use of a semi-trailer largely overcame the drawback of boiler length in a rigid vehicle.

REFINED CARRIAGES
THE STEAM CAR DREAM

The half-century between 1840 and 1890 can justly be called the Dark Ages of Motoring, for legal repression and public hostility had combined to eclipse the first bright coming of the steam carriage. But even in the darkness there were flashes of light – some dim and intermittent, some brilliant and sustained.

A few pioneers built steam carriages, for their own use or for sale to wealthy clients. In the late 1850s Thomas Rickett produced a handful of three-wheeled two-seaters, one of which was sold in 1858 to the Marquis of Stafford, and another to the Earl of Caithness. J. W. Boulton built several carriages between 1848 and 1860, and another early venture was the *Cornubia*, built by the Tangye brothers in 1868 and subsequently exported to India. Two companies, Yarrow and Hilditch and Garrett and Marshall, displayed private steam vehicles at the 1862 Great Exhibition in London.

New York saw its first steam carriage in the 1850s. The work of Richard Dudgeon, this looked like a liaison between a dwarf traction engine and two park benches, but it could carry 12 passengers at 14 mph (it was exhibited at the New York Crystal Palace in 1858, at the first New York Auto Show in 1900, and is now preserved in a Massachusetts museum).

The last, and the first, Bollée steam carriages. The 1885 16-seater double mail-coach bodied vehicle for the Marquis de Broc (left) was built by 18-year-old Amédée Bollée *fils*, while his father built *l'Obéissante* (right) in 1872–73 at the age of 39.

Quite the most remarkable figure of this period was Amédée Bollée, a bell-founder of Le Mans, who in 1871, at the age of 26, had set up a little workshop in the corner of the family factory to develop his personal dream—a practical horseless carriage.

Only two years later, his remarkable *l'Obéissante* was complete. Years ahead of its time, it featured independent front suspension with geometrically perfect steering and an iron chassis frame on which was mounted a metal panelled twelve-seater body. Each rear wheel was driven by a separate vee-twin engine; when *l'Obéissante* turned a corner, the steam supply to the engine on the inside of the curve was reduced to give the effect of a differential. There was also a separate two-speed gear incorporated in each power train. (The concept of a separate engine for each rear wheel was not new: W. H. James had patented a similar layout in 1824, while the road steamer built by Holt in 1866-67 had the 'driving wheels independently driven by two little double-cylinder engines'.)

After a couple of years of trials and modifications, Bollée judged that his creation was ready to be shown to a wider audience, so on October 9, 1875, he drove it to Paris, violating 75 traffic regulations on the way! These were quickly overlooked by the Prefect of Police after he had been driven along the boulevards and down the Champs-Elysées.

For a short while, *l'Obéissante* was the sensation of Paris, 'and became the subject of allusion in popular songs and plays, while its name was held up as an example to the Paris ladies'.

But advanced as it was, *l'Obéissante* marked a dead-end in automobile development. Bollée's next steam-car, *la Mancelle* (the girl from Le Mans) of 1878 was equally advanced in concept, for, with the engine at the front under a bonnet, driving the rear wheels by a shaft and side chains, it set the pattern for the layout of motorcars for years to come. Again, the front suspension was independent, this time by parallel leaf springs.

By 1880, limited production of *Mancelles*, fitted to option with *calèche* or *post-chaise* bodywork, was being undertaken by a staff of 50 workmen and a concessionaire-general, one Lecordier, was attempting to sell the vehicles. The price was a reasonable 12,000 francs, but there were few takers.

A licence to build *Mancelles* in Germany was acquired by a banker, Barthold Aerous, who planned grandiose bus services, not only in Germany and Austria, but also in Russia and Sweden. However, the Wöhlert locomotive factory, where the vehicles were being constructed, went bankrupt in 1883, after 22 Bollées had been built. Not only was this the end of the banker's schemes—Bollée, too, suffered as he never received the royalties due on his patents.

His post-*Mancelle* designs had shown the potential of his work. They were the closed carriage *la Nouvelle*, built for his father, and *la Rapide*, which placed control of the boiler under the direct command of the driver for the first time, instead of having a separate fireman/engineer. The secret lay in the provision of an automatic coal feed to the boiler; *la Rapide* lived up to its name when the second version reached a speed of 37 mph.

But Bollée's experiments had run him deeply into

This little tricar (below) was built by James Sumner of Leyland to the order of Theodore Carr, the Carlisle biscuit magnate, in 1895.

Right: the first fruit of the partnership between de Dion, Bouton and Trépardoux was this spidery little quadricycle, which was built in 1883.

debt, and he redirected his activities to bell founding, leaving the development of road vehicles to his elder son Amédée *fils*. In 1885, the eighteen-year-old Amédée *fils* built a neat little two-seater light car, and a grandiose sixteen-seat coach for the Marquis de Broc. Then he became intrigued by the infant internal-combustion engine. Like his father, Amédée *fils* was too far ahead of his time to be other than a technological success.

As the Bollées were fading from the scene, a meeting occurred in 1881 which resulted in the formation of one of the most famous companies of the pioneer days of motoring.

Count Albert de Dion was a young nobleman 'better known in society drawing rooms and even gaming rooms than in factories or workshops, but possessed of an imagination and faith in progress which was just looking for an outlet'. He had gone to the Giroux novelty shop in the Boulevard des Italiens to buy the favours for a ball he was organising, and was fascinated by a tiny model steam engine in the window.

He demanded to know who had made this beautiful toy, and was told that it was the work of two brothers-in-law, Bouton and Trépardoux, who scraped a living making toys for Giroux and more sophisticated showcase models for the Ducretet precision engineering company.

De Dion persuaded Bouton and Trépardoux to form a partnership with him, and they began work on a light steam carriage in a ramshackle house in the Rue Pergolese.

Left: the Scotte Steam Wagonette, which was built in Paris in 1892, is a surviving example of this make, which might otherwise be forgotten. The coal-fired vertical boiler is offset, with a twin-cylinder engine mounted alongside it. Drive to the rear axle is by a shaft and final belt drive.

Above: one of the earliest Stanley-Locomobile steamers. 'No smell, no gears, no rattle or vibration, no electricity, perfectly simple, simply perfect' according to its makers. 'As frail as a wicker willow lunch basket', according to one owner, Rudyard Kipling.

Their first vehicle appeared in 1883, fitted with a particularly efficient vertical boiler designed by Trépardoux who seems to have been the 'brains' of the enterprise, for he was later to design the 'De Dion' back axle for the company's heavy steam cars.

During the 1880s, however, development was restricted to light steam cars, some rear-steered four-wheeled *brakes*, but mostly tricycles, one of which, driven by the Count himself, won France's first motor race in Paris in April 1887. This wasn't such a fantastic feat, as the De Dion was the only competitor, and the Count drove round the course in solitary splendour, watched by a marvelling crowd.

But De Dion and Bouton were becoming increasingly preoccupied with the petrol engine, which promised to be a far superior form of propulsion for the light vehicles they planned to build. Trépardoux, seeing no future for this upstart power

unit, resigned in 1894, having designed the heavy drag which was to form the basis of the De Dion company's steam vehicles from then on.

Some of these drags were put to interesting uses — one, for example, pulled the first ever trailer caravan, built in 1896 for the Tsar's uncle, who planned to use it for hunting trips in the Caucasus. In the following year, an even more massive De Dion caravan outfit was constructed by the Parisian coachbuilder Jeantaud. The journalist who inspected this 'steam house', which was fully equipped to the extent of incorporating a bath and flush toilet, must have been having taxation problems, for his admiring comments began:

'At one time the dream of roving the country with a house free from the visits of the tax-gatherer would have seemed impossible of realisation, but in these days of autocars it has become an accomplished fact.'

But even with spectacular vehicles like this

Above: Sylvester H. Roper was an inventor of considerable
ability, although it is obvious from this poster that his
contemporaries regarded his steam vehicles as circus freaks.
Below: Copeland's Phaeton Moto-cycle of the late 1880s
was a motorized pedal tricycle. Despite its simple design,
and this advertisement, it was not marketed.

coming on to the road, De Dion and Bouton had
really lost interest in steam. Once their light four-
wheeled cars started selling in volume the steam
drags and lorries became first a sideline and then
vanished from the catalogue altogether. Nor was
the way of their going a dignified one, for the last
recorded sale of De Dion steamers was a fleet of
dungcarts for the Paris municipal authorities.

If De Dion and Bouton had aimed at building
ultra-light carriages, there were those who had
built lighter yet. Although the steam motorcycle
might seem a fairly impractical proposition, none-
theless it was as old as the bicycle itself, steam
velocipedes having appeared in 1868 in France and
America, developed independently by Perreaux
and Roper.

Sylvester H. Roper was an advocate of simplicity
and lightness, and had already built a handful of
spidery four-wheelers. His total output is believed
to be in the region of ten steamers, and he exhibited
both steam bicycles and buggies at fairs and circuses
in the Eastern United States. His velocipede could,
he claimed, 'be driven up any hill, and will out-
speed any horse in the world'.

On June 1, 1896, Roper dropped dead while
operating one of his steam bicycles on the Charles
River cycle track at Cambridge, Massachusetts.

In 1881 Lucius D. Copeland of Phoenix, Arizona,
had tried to fix a steam engine to a highwheeled
Columbia bicycle, with the idea of boosting the
rider's pedal power on hills and rough going, but the
project proved 'very inefficient and dangerous'.
Copeland then fitted a lightweight engine and
boiler to a Star bicycle, on which the small front
wheel steered and the rear wheel drove–this was
supposed to make the cycle ride more steadily. The
total weight of Copeland's powerpack was only
18 lb, and it was powerful enough to propel the
bicycle at 12 mph.

Copeland began exhibiting his machine in an
effort to secure financial backing to market it.
Eventually the Northrop Manufacturing Company
was formed, the finances being provided by San-
ford Northrop and two Philadelphia doctors named
Starkey and Palen.

Within three months of the formation of the
company, Copeland had a steam tricycle on the
road, with automatic water-level control, and automatic fire control dependent on boiler pressure;
operating the brake lever cut off the steam.

By 1890, design had progressed to the stage where
a tricycle phaeton was produced that could start
from cold in five minutes, reach 10 mph and cover
30 miles on a tank of water. Grandiose production
figures were claimed, but it is unlikely that any
'phaeton moto-cycles' ever got into public hands.

Above: a break-bodied de Dion steamer leads a rally of the notorious Harry Lawson's Motor Car Club through Warwickshire around 1897, and contravenes the Light Locomotives Act by emitting 'visible vapour'.

Below: Léon Serpollet at the controls of one of his earliest four-wheelers, prepared for the 1894 Paris–Rouen reliability trial—the first motoring competition.

Copeland, convinced that people would refuse to pay more than $500 (about £100) for a motor vehicle, saw little profit in the venture and faded from the scene.

And that, apart from a handful of Pearson-Cox machines built in 1912-13, was as near as the steam cycle ever got to being a commercial proposition. Henceforward the field was left to amateurs like James Sadler of Scotland who built a fast twin-cylinder steam bike in 1926, with a boiler operating at 700 psi. During tests, four pairs of Mr Sadler's trousers burst into flames, he sustained burns 'all over' and bystanders who were too near the flues had their eyebrows scorched off. Sadler, undeterred, continued experiments until 1940.

The major problem facing all the early light-weight constructors was that of providing a suitable boiler, one that was light and compact yet possessed adequate steaming capacity. The answer was provided by the invention of the flash boiler by Léon Serpollet in the 1880s.

The son of a blacksmith in rural France, Serpollet may have conceived his boiler by watching his father quench red-hot iron in water. Certainly that was the simile employed by H. Walter Staner in describing Serpollet's invention:

'So far as steam generation is concerned, the principle of the flash boiler may be likened to dropping water on a red-hot iron. A small stream of water is pumped through a coil of tubing, and this tubing is heated to an intense heat by the burners, so that almost as soon as the water enters it, it is 'flashed' into steam—that is to say, the process of boiling and steam generation is all gone through in a second, and the water which enters the coil of tubing at the bottom, issued from the top of the coil as high-pressure superheated steam.'

There had been few precedents to Serpollet's 'instantaneous steam generator'–John Payne had the first glimmerings of the idea in the 1730s, Jacob Perkins and Howard had conducted experiments in the 1820s, and in 1824 the American John Mc-Curdy had patented 'Steam Chambers' which perhaps approached Serpollet's concept the closest.

In 1876, when he was aged 18, Serpollet had built a crude steam tricycle, with everything bar engine and boiler made of wood. It did not use the flash boiler and proved completely unsuccessful. Eleven years later, in 1887, Serpollet, having set up a little workshop in the Rue des Cloys in Paris, built a little engine and coal-fired flash boiler out of scrap and fitted them to a second hand tricycle. For this machine, Serpollet was granted the first driving licence ever issued in Paris, in 1891.

Serpollet's next project was an improved three-wheeler with two seats and a more powerful engine driving the back axle through 4:1 reduction gears. At that time the French War Ministry were showing interest in motor traction, and Serpollet was asked to submit his car to an official test.

When the vehicle was running at 15 mph or so the soldier who was riding as observer asked Serpollet to demonstrate the effectiveness of the brakes. Serpollet pulled as hard as he could on the hand-brake . . . and the unfortunate soldier was pitched headlong out of the car.

Then, in 1889, Serpollet collaborated with Armand Peugeot to build a three-wheeler, on which Serpollet and his friend Ernest Archdeacon made one of the first motor tours, in January 1890.

Described as a 'stove nailed to a packing case', the car rattled out of Paris with no greater problem than a few frightened cab horses. Once the badly

Below: this 1910 Runabout is one of the most familiar Stanley steamers. The boiler is at the front, and its double-acting twin-cylinder engine fully enclosed underneath the car. It drove directly to the differential through a pair of spur gears. This runabout, which is one of the later examples, is preserved in the Henry Ford Museum.

Above: this 1920 Model 735-A Stanley looks like most of its high-class American contemporaries, although instead of a petrol engine the hood of course concealed a boiler. Engine and transmission followed the Runabout, in a layout which distinguished the breed. This Stanley once belonged to aircraft manufacturer Sir Richard Fairey.

rutted roads of the suburbs were reached the vibration caused 'nuts, small parts and pieces of coachwork to sow the soil'.

At almost every village Serpollet had to strip to his shirtsleeves and make replacement parts in the local blacksmith's shop, or lash the machinery together with bent wire.

'Suddenly, in the middle of a steep descent,' recalled Archdeacon, 'the steering bar snapped off short! The car rammed the bank, its nose against a tree. What to do? We could hardly call off the trip for so little.'

The damage couldn't be repaired on the spot, so Serpollet and Archdeacon lay down on the floor and leaned out, alternately punching the offending wheel to keep the car on course until the next village, four kilometres distant, was reached.

At the end of their 290 mile tour, not unnaturally, Serpollet and Archdeacon came home by train. The car came too, having gained 300 lb of surplus weight on the two-week trip, thanks to the number of repairs that had been carried out on it.

By now, Serpollet was beginning to receive orders from private customers for his latest four-wheeled model. Clients included chocolate millionaire Gaston Menier and Captain Klopstein of the Dragoons. The latter was wakened from a nap by the sound of his car being delivered, and was so excited that he rushed down to test-drive it stark naked!

According to *La Nature*, these models had twin-cylinder 4/6 hp engines under the driver's seat, with cranks at 180 degrees and a bore and stroke of 60.3 × 90.4 mm. A two-speed gear and chain final drive was fitted: on the top speed 16 mph could be attained on the flat, while the lower gear enabled a gradient of 1:12 to be climbed on a bad road surface with seven passengers aboard. Steam could be raised in a minimum of 20 minutes from cold, and water feed was automatic.

The car could be driven one-handed: a twist-grip on the steering bar opened or closed a valve which controlled the amount of water passing into the generator and returned the surplus to the feed tank. Should extra boiler pressure be needed to overcome some obstacle, the water supply could be augmented by a hand pump.

Coke was fed automatically to the rear-mounted boiler from hoppers; total fuel capacity was sufficient for an 18 mile journey, and enough water was carried for twice that distance.

But Serpollet had come to an impasse: he felt that solid fuel was unsuitable for a private carriage – it was too dirty for one thing – and he needed an alternative to the slide valves used in his engines. At the extremely high steam temperatures Serpollet was using, the valves would stick unless they were drenched in lubricant.

More importantly, Peugeot had withdrawn his support and was working on a petrol car, while Serpollet's other backers were more interested in steam trams. So steam trams it was for the rest of the 1890s, with only a handful of cars built to special order.

In 1898, however, Serpollet met a wealthy American, Frank L. Gardner, who provided him with finance not only to buy out his backers but to set up a new factory in the Rue Stendhal, Paris.

A new car, with a paraffin-fired flash boiler was developed; its flat-four engine followed petrol-engine practice, with poppet valves, which were more easily lubricated. It was, because of this, single-acting, and thus more easily comprehended by the average motorist; control, following Serpollet's theories, was almost automatic.

However, it was not the sophisticated Gardner-Serpollet that was to establish the steam car, but the relatively crude product of two identical twins from Newton, Massachusetts, F. E. and F. O. Stanley. Non-smoking, non-drinking, 'the best of

Top: Léon Serpollet's *Easter Egg* of 1902 had a 75 mph speed capability, and proved one of the fastest cars of its day in speed trials.

Above: Pelzer was a regular competitor in Gaillon hill climbs with a Gardner-Serpollet; here he is about to start in the 1904 event. The car's 'wind-cheating' body is noticeably less streamlined than the older *Easter Egg*.

Opposite: G. E. Milligen's 1904 15 hp *Roi des Belges* Gardner-Serpollet. This was an advanced car, and its importers loudly proclaimed its virtues by comparing it with a well-known rival . . .

Following pages: the Belgian-designed, British-built Turner-Miesse offered 'speed up to 50 mph, entirely at driver's discretion' at a claimed running cost of 'Less than ONE FARTHING per mile'.

good Yankees', the Stanleys had a natural flair for invention.

They started out by mass-producing violins, then invented a home generator for illuminating gas. Next they produced the dry photographic plate, and netted a fat fee by selling the patents to George Eastman's Kodak company. In between times, they built some of the first X-ray equipment.

In 1896, by way of a hobby, they began to build a steam car, although they 'knew but little about steam engines and less about boilers'.

The first engine and boiler built for them weighed over 150 lb more than the estimated weight of the entire car; but the vehicle ran quite successfully, apart from frightening the local horses.

Then the Stanleys designed a lightweight fire-tube boiler, wound round with piano wire to make it resistant to bursting. Between the autumn of 1897 and the summer of 1898 three more cars were built, incorporating the new boiler and a light engine built by J. W. Penny and Sons of Mechanic Falls, Maine.

After pestering F. O. Stanley for several months, a man named Methot from Boston managed to buy Stanley's car for $600. Stanley, knowing that he could build a better car at any time, accepted the offer. Up to that time there had been no thought of manufacturing the steamers for sale, but after F. E. Stanley had demonstrated a car at the 1898 Boston Automobile Show, 200 orders flooded in.

The brothers took over a bankrupt cycle works next to their dryplate factory and equipped it for production. But the fame of their products spread rapidly: only one of the two hundred cars was complete when John Brisben Walker, publisher of

Built in 1881 and still in running order 30 years later, the Parkyns-Bateman steam tricycle (above) was legislated off the roads as it failed to conform to the law's requirements relating to 'locomotives', or traction engines.

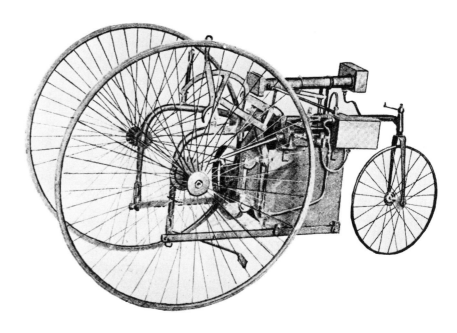

Below: at the end of 1900 Hubert W. Egerton drove this Locomobile from John O'Groats to Lands End. The journey took 11 days, and in 880 miles the boiler consumed more than 5 tons of water.

the *Cosmopolitan* magazine, offered to buy the entire Stanley automobile company, and asked the brothers to name their price.

To scare him off they told him that they wanted $250,000.

'Exactly the figure I had in mind, a quarter of a million,' he said, and wrote out a $500 cheque as deposit.

Walker subsequently sold a half-share in the business to one Amzi Lorenzo Barber. Within a fortnight the partners had disagreed and separated. Walker's half of the business became the Mobile Company of America; Barber's the Locomobile Company of America. The products of both companies were virtually identical, but it was the Locomobile which enjoyed the greatest success. It was the first volume-produced car, and by 1902 the company claimed to have produced half the 8,000 motor cars then running in the United States, and to operate the largest and most modern steam automobile factory in the world.

The very board of directors read like a clarion call: 'Amzi Lorenzo Barber, President; Le Droict Langdon Barber, Vice-President; Samuel T. Davis, Jr, Treasurer; Freeland O. Stanley, Francis E. Stanley, General Managers'.

And the company's claims for its products were no less impressive:

'The placing of the "Locomobile" carriage on the market opens up a new era. It brings within the reach of the man of ordinary means the power to travel in his own conveyance at a rate of speed limited only by the character of the road, at a cost that is almost nominal.

'It is a demonstrated success. A single carriage has been tested in the United States over runs aggregating 10,000 miles, without appreciable injury. The movement of the machine and its workmanlike construction have attracted the widest admiration wherever shown.

'The requisite of being able to climb the steepest road gradient is one of the most important. The "Locomobile" can climb a gradient of 1 in 7 with ease, and has actually climbed a gradient of 1 in 3!

'The "Locomobile" can be got ready by an expert in less than five minutes, and takes from five to ten minutes to get up to its fullest power.

'The "Locomobile" is operated without jolt or jar, or vibration of any kind.

'When running along a level, or nearly level road, the machinery makes absolutely no noise. When climbing a gradient a slight puffing is audible, but nothing in the least degree objectionable.

'The art of operating the "Locomobile" is easily and quickly mastered by a man or woman of fair intelligence, and a few hours' instruction for a couple of days will give a full comprehension of the carriage, and its operation in every particular.

'Its light and graceful appearance is undeniable.

'The claim made for the "Locomobile" carriage is that it has no equal on the world's markets.'

But the truth was not quite up to the publicity. While the Locomobile was a creditable effort for a car built as a hobby, it was not really up to the rigours of everyday motoring.

Among those who suffered was Rudyard Kipling, who, in a letter to his American publisher, signed himself 'Yours Locomobiliously'. His car was described as 'a holy terror . . . just now her record is one of eternal and continuous breakdown . . . she apparently must be taken to pieces every time anything goes wrong with her . . . It is true that she is noiseless, but so is a corpse, and one does not get much fun out of a corpse!

'It isn't as if we wanted her for long tours—isn't as if we ever tried to get more than ten miles an hour out of her. We got her for a carriage—a refined and ladylike carriage—and we treat her on that basis. Her lines are lovely; her form is elegant; the curves of her buggy-top are alone worth the price of admission, but, as a means of propulsion she is a nickel-plated fraud.'

However, there was little hope of the Locomobile's inherent faults being rectified, as the Stanleys' connection with the company was in name only. They were busy developing an improved model which they planned to produce under their own name when they were free from their contractual obligation not to produce steam cars in opposition to Locomobile (the specified period was only a year!) and were not interested in revising an already outmoded design.

Locomobile gave up the steam car for petrol in 1903 and the Stanleys bought back their own manufacturing rights for a mere $20,000. They promptly granted licences to use two of their patents to the White Company for $15,000: a factory, their patents, and a quarter of a million dollars—not bad for $5,000!

Furthermore, the Stanleys preserved their good name through the Locomobile affair—other companies inspired by the runaway sales of the Locomobile, had tried to cash in by producing Chinese copies of that little steamer. Among these were the Binney and Burnham, the Brecht, the Century, the Conrad, Covert, Eclipse, Foster, Geneva, Grout, Howard, Hudson, Kensington, Milwaukee, Prescot, Reading, Richmond, Rochester, Skene, Stearns and Sunset automobiles. All were doomed to early deaths, few lingering on into 1905, save for those who changed their horse-power in midstream and went over to internal combustion.

One of the best of the light American steamers was the twin-cylinder Toledo, which was in production between 1900 and 1902. This 1900 model belongs to P. G. Newens, who spent 4000 hours restoring it after it was found hanging in the rafters of a rope factory. Its neat engine compartment is shown opposite.

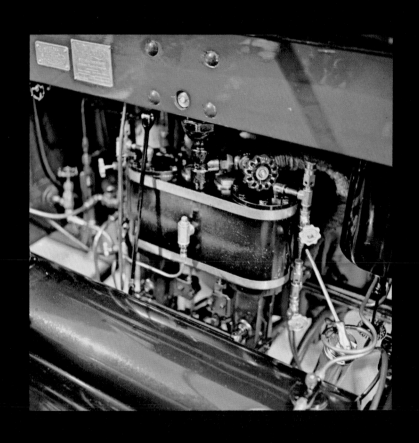

At the 1905 Ormond Beach race meet, Louis Ross drove *Teakettle* (no 4) with its two 10 hp Stanley engines along a measured mile in 38 seconds, a speed of 94.75 mph. The long-bonneted freak behind it (no 2) is Herbert L. Bowden's eight-cylinder 110 mph *Flying Dutchman*, which was powered by two 60 hp Mercedes engines mounted in tandem.

The Stanleys, however, kept on going with their improved design, which had its twin-cylinder engine geared directly to the back axle in a layout that would not change during the remainder of the marque's long life. Particularly covetable was the 'Gentleman's Speedy Roadster' which, in its 30 hp form, could touch 75 mph, although the boiler capacity was not sufficient for such speeds to be sustained.

In 1905, standard Stanley engines with increased boiler capacity were fitted in low streamlined bodies – probably the first car bodies to be developed by wind-tunnel tests – for attempts on speed records. *Teakettle*, *Beetle* and *Wogglebug* were the three most famous names. *Beetle* (alias *Wogglebug*) exceeded 127 mph on Ormond Beach, Florida, in January 1906; a year later, the driver, Fred Marriott, attempted to break his own record, but, at a speed estimated at 150 mph, the light Stanley became airborne, flipped over and was smashed to fragments, although Marriott escaped with his life.

The Stanleys never built another 'racer' – they thought there were too many risks involved, although the brothers themselves were fast, reckless drivers. Accused in court of driving a racing Stanley on the roads at 'nearly 60 mph', F. E. pleaded 'not guilty' although the evidence against him was clear. Asked to explain his plea he replied: 'I plead not guilty to going 60 miles an hour. When I passed the officer my speedometer showed I was going 87 miles an hour!'

It was this love of speed which proved F. E.'s undoing. Breasting a hill at high speed, he found two farm wagons drawn up across the road so that their drivers could chat in comfort. Swerving to avoid them, he was killed. Only a few months earlier, in May 1918, the brothers had retired at the age of 70, and their company had been taken over by a new group led by Prescott Warren. The later Stanley cars were large and staid, looking rather like old-fashioned petrol cars.

Mr F. O. retired to Colorado for his health, and spent his remaining years running his luxury hotel in Estes Park and whittling violins.

In 1916 the Stanleys had at last bowed to convention and fitted a condensor to their cars to conserve water – a move they had resisted because New England was amply endowed with horsetroughs. Anyway, reasoned the brothers, no one would want to travel more than forty miles in a day, so that was the capacity of the water and fuel tanks.

The change had, however, been forced by warnings from the Chicago and Boston city authorities that Stanleys would not be allowed within city limits unless steps were taken to curtail the clouds of uncondensed fog which formed behind them in damp or cold weather, restricting visibility for following drivers. (This departure did nothing to boost flagging sales.) The Stanley company ceased production in 1927, although spasmodic attempts were made to revive it. Average motorists did not mourn the passing of the Stanley but dogs did, for the cars emitted a high-pitched whistle which attracted them, so that the Stanley owner was always guaranteed a canine cortege.

The biggest rival of the Stanley in the first decade of the century was the White, built by a well-known sewing machine manufacturer of Cleveland, Ohio. The first Whites, built in 1900, were conventional steam buggies on similar lines to the Locomobile, but in 1903 came a new model with a front-mounted twin-cylinder compound engine, a condensor in the 'radiator' position and a 'semi-flash' steam generator, which 'had none of the disadvantages peculiar to a boiler'.

Unlike the pure flash boiler, the White unit had reserve capacity which could be called on in an emergency. This made the car especially competi-

tive in short distance speed events, and as early as 1901 the 'fleet little White Stanhopes' were 'beating the large gasoline cars in hollow fashion'.

Like Stanley, White believed in the advertising value of competition success, and special racers, such as *Turtle*, *Bob*, and *Snail* were built.

But the most famous of all the White racers was *Whistling Billy*, built early in 1905 for the racing driver Webb Jay, who commented in the *White Bulletin*:

'Judging from the victories which White stock cars, both stripped and in touring condition, have constantly won in track competition, I have always shared in the notion that a White car built especially for track racing would be able to compete on a little better than even terms with anything else on

Fred Marriott (in duster and goggles) poses with one of the Stanley brothers before setting up his record speed of 127.66 mph in the Stanley *Beetle* in 1906. Trying to better

this speed in the following year, Marriott crashed at around 150 mph and was lucky to escape alive. The engine (on the left of the lower photograph) was notably compact.

Top: probably the most desirable of the Stanleys was the 1908 Gentleman's Speedy Roadster, which was capable of more than 80 mph in standard trim.

Above: the driver of this 1901 White Stanhope looks much less confident of his part of the equipage than the splendid figure in the petrol-engined launch . . .

Left: this terrain looks far too rugged for the dainty wheels and the suspension of this 1901 Locomobile

Another photograph of a 1901 White Stanhope, which
suggests that it was a far from ideal touring machine – apart
from the lack of range which was always a drawback of
early steam cars, its luggage-carrying arrangements were
awkward in the extreme. Total sales of the 1901 model,
which had tiller steering and underfloor twin-cylinder
engine, were 193.

four wheels. Accordingly, when the White Company this spring constructed such a car and entrusted the driving of it to me, I felt that it would soon be demonstrated that steam is supreme on the track, as it long ago showed itself to be upon the road.

'The White racer is equipped with an engine identical with those in the regular White car. The

generator, however, is of greater capacity and supplies steam at a higher pressure than in the touring car. The car steers from the left-hand side, power is transmitted from the engine to the rear axle by means of a shaft, and everything is hung close to the ground in order to bring the centre of gravity as low as possible.

'The first car competed in the opening races at

The Incomparable White. This 1904 model, which had a compound engine, could run for 100 miles on one filling of water and petrol, and its makers claimed that 'its operating parts are so arranged that a lady need have no fear of soiling even a glove in running the car'. Apparently it also had practical virtues in the eyes of an unidentified public utilities department.

Morris Park, New York, on May 20. On that day I drove the car an exhibition mile in 53 sec, equalling the former track record.

'Many people have asked me to describe the sensations one experiences when travelling at the rate of over 70 mph. Well, going down the stretches is comparatively tame. If you were fastened down somewhere and a 70-mile-an-hour cyclone were sweeping by you, you would get some idea of the way the wind whistles past the face of one travelling in a car at the same rate of speed. But the turns are quite a different proposition. For every track and every car there is a certain speed at which the car would topple over on the turns in obedience to the laws of Nature. The task of the driver of a fast machine is to take his car around the turns at a speed—as near as his judgment tells him—which is close to this limit, but still a shade on the safe side. If there is a car ahead, the driver is travelling through a cloud of dust, with only now and then a rift through which he can see the fence, and the task becomes somewhat more formidable.'

Certainly such exercises contributed to the impressive sales figures achieved by White: in 1906 they produced 1,500 vehicles, and their tourers were used by no less a person than Theodore Roosevelt, President of the United States.

Unlike the early Stanleys, the Whites were quite suitable for long-distance touring. In 1910 P. G. Konody drove one through France, across the Alps to Italy and returned, via Austria and Germany. His car was 'a 30 hp White Steam—noiseless, running as smoothly as a sledge, equipped with a comfortable touring body and luggage carrier; and, above all, a splendid hill-climber. She seemed positively to enjoy flying uphill, and expressed her pleasure by a gentle, musical chirping sound'.

The only troubles seem to have been a propensity for running out of fuel in awkward places—hardly the car's fault—and some minor lamp and tyre problems.

But White saw the writing on the wall as their steam-powered contemporaries faded from the scene. In 1910 a petrol model made its bow, although the company soft-pedalled it in their advertising at first:

'Someone said that the White Company, having placed upon the sales market the White Petrol Car, would discontinue the manufacture of the White Steam Car. Therefore it might interest you to know that not only in America, but also in England, the White Company has sold more steam cars this season than ever before and at the present time has a greater number of steam cars being completed in London—right out in Camden Town—than at any previous time in its history. Come and see for yourself.'

Top: built in Paris, the 1902 Chaboche steamer could seat six to eight passengers, had a twin-cylinder engine, and would burn either coal or coke.

Centre: one of the last cars to be built by Pearson-Cox, this 1913 15 hp tourer featured a semi-flash boiler and a three-cylinder engine.

Above: the Morriss-London steam car was a real rarity, for only four were built between 1908 and 1914. This one was probably the last to be made. It has a twin-cylinder engine.

But it was all so much flannel. By the end of 1911 the company's output was purely petrol, and by 1918 they had abandoned private cars entirely in favour of trucks.

In Europe the steam car had faded away even more rapidly. Initially, Léon Serpollet's cars had promised great things, and his racing cars could even show the much-vaunted Mercedes a thing or two. In 1902 his streamlined *Easter Egg* had covered a kilometre in 29.8 seconds to become – briefly – the fastest car in the world at a speed of 75 mph.

Serpollet told reporters:

'I knew the car was all right and I knew how to get the maximum out of it. I was quite calm at the moment of departure: a second or two later I was conscious of a sensation of speed that can only be called fearful. In all my previous experiences I have been able to fairly well calculate the speed at which I was going by the whistling of the air in my ears, but this time I heard and saw nothing.'

But Serpollet was a sick man, slowly dying of consumption, and his company reached its zenith around 1904 when 15 hp and 40 hp cars were introduced, with the refinement of a separate steam donkey engine. This operated the steam and water pumps independently of the speed of travel, albeit at the cost of 10-15 per cent greater fuel consumption.

To motoring writer A. B. Filson Young the Serpollet was 'the aristocratic steam car. Its workmanship is beyond reproach . . . I should not describe it, however, as a cheap or economical car, nor has any attempt been made to make a cheap car of it. It is suitable for those who can afford to pay for reputation and for the distinction of an undisputed prestige'.

However, the distinction and prestige rested squarely on Léon Serpollet: he *was* the Gardner-Serpollet company, and when he died in February 1907, the heart went right out of the business, although Darracq, who took it over, did build some steam commercials.

British steam cars were even less successful. The Turner-Miesse, superficially similar to the Serpollet, first appeared in 1902, and, on paper at least, survived until 1913, giving it an equal life-span to the White; it outlived the Belgian Miesse on which it was based by more than seven years. Other companies, like Pearson-Cox and Morriss-London, had very short lives, and only built a handful of cars (the Cox half of Pearson-Cox subsequently invented the splendid Cox-Atmos carburetter).

But if the steam car was dead in Europe, in America it was a mighty long time lying down. During the 1920s numerous makers appeared briefly on the scene, most producing only one or two cars and relieving shareholders of a few thousand dollars before vanishing into oblivion.

Only one make enjoyed any lasting success during that period – and that was a *succès d'éstime* rather than any financially rewarding venture. This was the Doble, built between 1924 and 1932 in Emeryville, California, by Abner Doble, who had already designed the flash-boilered Doble-Detroit of 1918-22.

Doble's factory at Emeryville was based on the American Rolls-Royce works at Springfield, Massachusetts, and his aim was to achieve the same standard of finish. The four-cylinder compound engine of the Doble was built in unit with the back axle casing. It was no mean performer: 'This engine, which is simple and sturdy in its construction, operates with a velvet smoothness unknown in the internal combustion engine. There is no vibration or noise. Yet it has such power that the car will accelerate from 1 to 75 miles an hour in a few seconds . . . such power that the car will climb any hill upon which the rear wheels can maintain traction'.

Doble aimed at making his steamers as automatic as possible: the burner was ignited automatically, and, thanks to a venturi booster blower, could raise a full head of steam in under a minute. Enthusiasts claimed it would run on anything combustible, from coal dust to petrol. But Doble's quest for perfection was fanatical – all joints in the engine were metal-to-metal, lapped in without gaskets, and the amount of hand work involved meant that his cars were expensive. At twice the price of a Rolls-Royce, the Doble could only be afforded by millionaires (Howard Hughes had two!). The paradox was that in making the steam car as easy to operate as possible, Doble had to make its mechanism highly complicated. Henry Ford could make a car that anyone could drive, and sell it for $260; Abner Doble couldn't do it under $8,000. Ford sold over fifteen million Model Ts; Doble's output was just forty-two cars.

During the 1930s the steam car ceased to be a commercial production and became the preserve of enthusiasts, most of whom spent a great deal of money to produce steam vehicles that were less satisfactory than the petrol cars they were intended to supplant.

There were some notable exceptions: J. Roy Hunt of Los Angeles built a futuristic motor caravan that looked like something out of Flash Gordon (a shower with hot water laid on was a side benefit of steam power!). And the Besler brothers of San Francisco consistently experimented – they eventually took over the Doble factory at Emeryville and in 1933 they achieved the one and only trouble-free

Top: the 1902 Chaboche light vis-a-vis used liquid fuel – petrol or paraffin. Its twin-cylinder engine drove through a shaft.

Centre: this 1925 Murphy-bodied Doble belonged to William J. Besler, who took over Doble's Emeryville factory in the 1930s.

Above: power plant of the Doble, which could raise a sufficient head of steam to start from cold in 30–45 seconds. Claimed cruising speed of this 'perfect' steam car was 75 mph

flight in a steam-powered aircraft, fitting a 90 hp vee-twin engine of their own make in a Travelair biplane.

Doble himself went to Europe when his business closed down, acting as technical consultant to Sentinel in England and Henschel in Germany.

Although his work was mostly concerned with buses and trucks, he did find time to convert a Mercedes tourer to steam; Herman Goering was among those who rode in it.

In the petrol rationing of the war years and after, steam received a fair amount of publicity, as owners

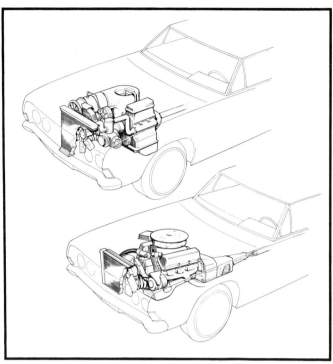

Above: design studies by General Motors (left) and Ford (right) proved the feasibility of installing steam power plants in the engine compartments of modern cars.

Below: the Australian architect Gene van Grecken conceived his Gvang as a complete entity, and unveiled it at the 1972 Sydney Motor Show. A computer is built in to monitor the burner output of the flash boiler and full

power can be developed from cold in 30 seconds. The unique oscillating piston engine has a claimed output of 400 bhp at 3500 rpm, giving this prototype a theoretical top speed of 200 mph.

Van Grecken spent over £300,000 on the development of the prototype, but his initial production plans are for 60 bhp city commuter cars, comparable in price with four-cylinder internal combustion engined cars.

of steam cars were able to run them on paraffin, which was not subject to restrictions. Newspapers commented on the revival of old Stanleys and Dobles, and even the almost extinct steam commercial made a brief comeback.

I remember that our local coal merchants brought their fleet of Fodens out of retirement around 1945-46, and still recall the magnificent sight of a chocolate brown Foden overtype thrashing up the hill where I lived at the time.

After the war and the rationing, however, the petrol car had it all its own way, and the steamer was only to be seen at antique car events.

There were the usual optimistic forecasts that steam was about to make a comeback but somehow it never did. A plan to provide the teeming millions of China with cheap mass-produced steam cars was nipped in the bud when Chairman Mao took over.

Robert Paxton McCulloch planned a modernised Doble in the early 1950s, and Abner Doble was engaged as design consultant, but the project was arbitrarily dropped in 1954.

In England, Singer Motors experimented with a steam conversion of their SM 1500, but denied its existence when quizzed by the press; Leo J. Shorter, their chief designer, had been experimenting with light steam engines for some years. The project, not unnaturally, was still-born. More recently another prominent car designer, Sir Alec Issigonis, has been toying with steam cars, proposing a steam version of his famous Mini.

But during the 1960s, interest in steam power quickened again. The growing concern with the atmospheric pollution created by the internal combustion engine prompted the major American car producing companies to take an interest in alternative methods of propulsion.

In 1966 Ford ran emission tests on a prototype steam car constructed by the Williams Engine Company, and discovered that the carbon monoxide level put out by the engine was a thirtieth of the current permissible level: the Williams Company, with well over 25 years' experience in steam, used a modified Ford chassis. The Williams four-cylinder engine operated on a patented cycle: a single-acting uniflow engine with poppet valves, it compressed the residual steam in the cylinder to a ratio of 26:1, when it reached a temperature of 1,569 deg F; new steam was then admitted from the boiler at 1,000 deg F, forming a 1,300 deg F mixture, and eliminating any tendency for steam to condense in the cylinder. The flash boiler could generate enough steam to drive the car within 20 seconds of ignition from cold, and the car was said to be capable of 100 mph.

While Ford is still keeping a watching brief on steam developments of this kind, the company has made no recent announcement about progress in this field. In 1966 the Williams brothers began marketing kits to convert petrol cars to steam.

A steam-powered family car was proposed by the STP oil additive corporation in 1969—the head of STP, Andy Granatelli, and his chief engineer had gained useful experience working on the Paxton Phoenix. Their design incorporated a 'jet condenser', which promised useful water economies, but the project was still-born.

Another project, which got under way in 1972, involved the Chrysler Corporation, in a joint programme with the Steam Engine Systems Corporation of Newton, Massachusetts, and three other companies, Ricardo, Esso Research and Bendix. The aim was to develop, assemble and test 'a complete engine system capable of powering a standard passenger saloon'.

General Motors, on the other hand, have progressed through various feasibility studies, one a curiously ill-conceived uniflow power unit weighing 450 lb more than the petrol engine it supplanted, and the other a Besler-designed engine of rather more promise, before turning to collaborating with Bill Lear in the development of a steam turbine engine which began trials in a bus chassis during 1972.

Lear is the most colourful figure in modern steam development, having dissipated $11 million of the fortune he amassed from his successful aircraft company in reaching the present state of development of his power unit.

In 1969 Lear built an 800 bhp four-wheel drive racing steamer intended for the Indianapolis 500, but the car was not readied in time for the race—and in any case, it did not comply with the regulations. At the same time, a limited production run of $30,000 'Learmousines' for luxury carriage trade was projected.

Like the Indianapolis venture, Lear's plans for providing California's Highway Patrol with steam-powered pursuit cars came to nothing, because of technical or financial troubles, but the bus engine seems to work well, out-performing the diesel it replaced. The Lear turbine operates most efficiently at 40,000-60,000 rpm and needs a complex automatic transmission layout to operate successfully; nevertheless, Lear hopes that engines of this type can be produced commercially to compete with diesels.

However, there is no indication that steam power units are likely to appear in private cars in the immediate future unless some unforeseen legislation forces the car makers' corporate hands.

LIVE STEAM

ENGINES IN PRESERVATION

As the fire went out of the steam age in the 1930s, hundreds of traction engines were scrapped for no better reason than that they were unfashionable. More were cut up for salvage during the Second World War.

But here and there a driver would buy his engine at a knockdown price for old times' sake or an enthusiast would acquire an engine to save it from the breakers – and, of course, there were people who kept on using their traction engines because they saw no point in replacing something that was still perfectly serviceable. Little effort was made to show these preserved engines to the public until 1950, when farmer Arthur Napper, of Appleford, Berkshire, challenged his friend Miles Chetwynd-Stapleton to a 'one-mile iron-horse steeplechase'. Their mounts were, respectively, a 1902 Marshall engine called *Old Timer* and a 1918 Aveling and Porter, *Lady Grove*.

Old Timer won, but the significant aspect of the contest was that a sizeable crowd had turned out to watch it – and this gave steam enthusiasts the idea of holding regular traction engine rallies.

Eventually, in 1954, the National Traction Engine Club was formed, appropriately with Arthur Napper as its President. Today it is the premier organisation in its field, and has more than 30 area clubs affiliated to it.

A code of practice for the organisation of steam rallies was drawn up, with the emphasis on safety, and many engines were acquired by private owners and restored to immaculate condition – far better than they had known when in service.

The rallies grew in size and popularity, but until recently the demonstrations given by the engines were restricted to musical chairs, obstacle races and other activities not entirely suitable for vehicles of their age and dignity. In the 1960s efforts were made to organise steam fairs. Here the engines could be seen working in much the same way as they had when new – showmen's engines were used to generate power for the roundabouts and rides, ploughing engines gave demonstrations, traction engines drove threshing machines and saw benches. Several such events are organised each year, where the general public can experience the esoteric delights of gallopers, steam yachts and bioscopes, while over the hiss and thud of the engines comes the cheerful blare of the fairground organ.

A circa 1915 Case engine surrounded by modern Case agricultural machinery at an agricultural show in America (above) contrasts with one of its English counterparts, the 1919 Foster *Duke of Wellington*, at a steam rally (right). The Foster spent most of its working life in Denbighshire.

Left: driver's eye view of a compound traction engine on the road. One wonders whether the boiler-cleaning instruction is taken seriously nowadays, although boiler safety inspections certainly are.
Above: *Morning Cloud* is a 1926 Aveling & Porter tractor which was originally supplied to Kent County Council.
Following pages: *Toby* is a 1926 Babcock & Wilcox roller in preservation. The Babcock name was used on the last steam rollers built by the famous traction engine makers Clayton & Shuttleworth, of Titanic Works, Lincoln. A driver's life in the heyday of steam was hard, but modern enthusiasts find obvious contentment in a sweetly-running engine . . .

Similar rallies are organised in America by the Rough and Tumble Engineers Historical Association, preserving and operating steam engines.

And, of course, there is the Steam Automobile Club of America, whose members not only preserve and restore antique steamers but actively pursue the development of the modern steam car. At their meets early Locomobiles and Stanleys mingle with one-off specials and exciting new power units like the Gibbs-Hosick Elliptocline produced by members. One enthusiast achieved the best of most possible worlds by making an antique car out of a 1921 Dodge chassis, a model 735 Stanley engine and miscellaneous parts of an American La France fire engine–'it looked a little like every antique car you've ever seen and goes like a banshee', commented the SACA magazine.

Such people would find their feelings summed up by Filson Young's 1906 comments that 'a steam car provides a pleasanter and more graceful occupation than . . . a petrol car'.

'The whole management of the two is different; a more loving, more personal care is necessary for steam; it needs more delicate and imaginative handling; its disorders are slighter, less obscure, more human than those of the petrol engine.'

And its appeal, it would seem, greater than it has ever been.